STEWARDSHIP IN THE NEW TESTAMENT CHURCH

Stewardship in the New Testament Church

A Study in the Teachings of Saint Paul Concerning Christian Stewardship

by

HOLMES ROLSTON

Pastor of the West Avenue Presbyterian Church
Charlotte, North Carolina

WIPF & STOCK · Eugene, Oregon

Wipf and Stock Publishers
199 W 8th Ave, Suite 3
Eugene, OR 97401

Stewardship in the New Testament Church
A Study in the Teachings of Saint Paul
concerning Christian Stewardship
By Rolston, Holmes
ISBN 13: 978-1-4982-9860-5
Publication date 6/2/2016
Previously published by John Knox Press, 1946

THIS BOOK IS DEDICATED TO MY SISTER

Frances Rolston

WHO HAS ALWAYS BEEN MY INSPIRATION

IN HER DEDICATION OF LIFE AND HER

STEWARDSHIP OF POSSESSIONS

Acknowledgments

I WISH to thank Dr. Harry S. Myers, Secretary of the United Stewardship Council of the Churches of Christ of the United States and Canada, for reading the manuscript of this book and for making a number of suggestions as to content and form. These suggestions have been adopted without exception.

I wish to thank Rev. H. S. Minnich, D. D., Chairman of the Committee on Education and Publications of the United Stewardship Council, for his evaluation of the manuscript.

A similar expression of thanks is due to Rev. Patrick H. Carmichael, Ph. D., Director of Leadership Education of the Presbyterian Church in the United States; to Rev. J. G. Patton, Jr., D. D., Secretary of the General Assembly's Committee on Stewardship of the Presbyterian Church in the United States; to Rev. B. K. Tenney, of the Executive Committee of Home Missions of the Presbyterian Church in the United States; to Dr. Herman J. Sweet, Director of Leadership Education, International Council of Religious Education; to Dr. J. S. Armentrout, Dean of Presbyterian College of Christian Education, Chicago; and to Dr. J. Fisher Simpson, Director of Leadership Education of the Methodist Church.

I wish to thank Rev. Mark A. Dawber, D. D., Executive Secretary of the Home Missions Council of North Carolina, both for helpful suggestions given while I was writing the book and for the Foreword which he has so graciously contributed.

I wish also to express to Miss Margaret Smith, of Charlotte, North Carolina, my appreciation for her very efficient work in the preparing of this manuscript for publication.

Unless otherwise indicated, all quotations of Scripture in this book are taken from the King James Version. Quotations from the American Standard Version are used by permission of the International Council of Religious Education.

HOLMES ROLSTON

Foreword

It is an honor to be invited to write a word of commendation on this book by Dr. Rolston. I have been interested in various programs of stewardship and in the stewardship movement, and for a long time have felt that we needed a broader Biblical and more dynamic treatment of stewardship. This book in my judgment meets the need. Dr. Rolston brings to the discussion a scholarly attitude, a historical and Biblical analysis, and, what is even more important, a very practical application.

Although the central concern is that of Paul's teachings on stewardship, the book is in a very real sense the essence of the teachings of Jesus on stewardship. Paul was without doubt the one man who could come nearest to interpreting the stewardship teachings of Jesus, and for that reason, I suspect, he was selected by Dr. Rolston for this study. Without detracting from the Old Testament values for stewardship, I believe it is only fair to say that, in the light of the new content and meaning of religion that developed with the coming of Jesus, it would follow that stewardship would also take on new meaning and larger content. It is this that Dr. Rolston brings out so clearly as he analyzes the teachings of Paul.

Our churches are sadly in need of the stewardship program that is inevitable if this book is given serious study. I can think of no greater contribution that could be made to the whole cause of missions, both at home and abroad, than the study of this volume in all the churches. The present crisis in world affairs—nay, the crisis in the church itself—calls for a new dedication of life and substance to the cause of Christ. This is the objective that I find running through these pages, and the least I can do is to commend it to all those who are concerned that the church achieve a new and greater impetus as it must now meet the larger demands that are upon it.

Mark A. Dawber

Preface

"THERE is a book in the teachings of Saint Paul concerning Christian stewardship." This statement was made during the delivery of the lecture on "The Economic Order" as one of a series of lectures on "The Social Message of the Apostle Paul" which I gave as the Sprunt Lectures of 1942 at Union Theological Seminary of Richmond, Virginia. I made this statement because I was conscious at the time that the insights concerning Christian stewardship which were to be found within the writings of the Apostle Paul could not be treated adequately in one lecture. But at the time I had no intention of attempting to develop this material into a book.

At the close of this lecture, the Rev. Patrick H. Carmichael, Ph. D., the Director of Leadership Education in the Presbyterian Church in the United States, said that he had felt for a long time the need for a book that would deal with stewardship against the background of the thought of the Apostle Paul. A few months later he graciously extended to me the invitation to give the lectures at the Bible Hour of the Montreat Leadership School in July of 1943. In his invitation, he requested that I develop in these lectures the teachings of Paul concerning stewardship. This book contains the substance of these lectures.

A word of explanation needs to be given concerning the title, *Stewardship in the New Testament Church.* My first plan was to give the book the title "The Apostle Paul Preaches Christian Stewardship." On the advice of the publishers I have adopted the title under which the book now appears. This title is justified in that while the book undertakes to give an exposition of the teachings of Paul concerning Christian stewardship, it is at the same time a study of the practice of stewardship in the New Testament church. It is to the book of Acts and the letters of Paul that we must always go as the major sources of our knowledge of the way in which the church that is reflected in the New Testament interpreted for her members the meaning of Christian stewardship. As the New Testament church is both the source and the norm of the church today, the study of stewardship as it was actually practiced in this church is certain to be of value for the guidance of the church in the modern world.

HOLMES ROLSTON

Table of Contents

CHAPTER I

The Old Testament Background

Paul Roots in the Old Testament

NO man ever grows up in complete independence of the social culture in which he lives. The Old Testament prophets, for example, rise above the life of Israel as a whole. The prophets are able to criticize the world in which they live. They are able to see that world as it is called in judgment by the righteousness of God. But the great prophets of Israel could not have arisen outside of Israel. Amos would not have been understood at all if he had suddenly appeared in Syria to condemn the social life of Syria as it fell short of the plumb line of the righteousness of Jehovah. Men like Isaiah and Micah could not have arisen in the eighth century in Egypt. And even Jesus came in the fullness of time and of the seed of Abraham. He could not have been understood if Israel had not prepared the world for His coming.

The Apostle Paul is no exception to this general rule. He was raised in the home of an orthodox Jew. He received his education at the hands of Gamaliel. His writings reveal an amazing knowledge of the Old Testament. When Paul became a Christian his attitudes concerning the Old Testament must have undergone a tremendous transformation. But the Old Testament still remained to him the word of God. As a Christian thinker, Paul's thought was determined by the meaning for him of the word of God which was revealed in Jesus Christ. But the background of his thought was to be found in the Old Testament.

It is appropriate, therefore, that in a book which seeks to study the teachings of Paul concerning Christian stewardship we should give an opening chapter to a consideration of the teachings concerning stewardship which are to be found in the Old Testament. Such a study does not attempt in any way to be exhaustive. It is intended merely as an introduction to the study of the thought of Paul. It is attempted because a background study such as this is essential to an understanding of the thought of the Apostle Paul on this subject.

way in which the prophets of the Lord must have stood in Israel for the right of every man to retain his ancestral inheritance.

Part of the breakdown of Israel's life in the eighth century lay in the way in which at this time the land laws of Israel were defied and the peasants were driven from their land. Because of this, the prophet Micah cries out against those who "covet fields, and seize them; and houses, and take them away: and they oppress a man and his house, *even a man and his heritage*."[7]

Who Owns the Earth?

No one would attempt to apply the land laws of Israel to the complex conditions of modern society. But the fundamental idea which underlies these laws is sound. The question as to who owns the land is still a vital question. The socialist would say that the earth and its resources belong to the people as a whole and not to the individuals who happen to have seized them. A capitalistic society is based on the private ownership of wealth. But this right is not an unlimited right. There must be set over against it the understanding that the earth and its resources belong ultimately to God. In this relation man is steward, not owner. An uncontrolled individualism needs to be constantly reminded of the divine ownership of the earth and its resources.

The Law Against the Taking of Interest

We would pass beyond the purposes of this chapter if we should try to study in detail the prohibition of the taking of interest on money in the Old Testament. The real force of this law has been obscured by the fact that in the King James Version the word usury is used to translate the Hebrew word for interest. Usury has come to mean in our speech today the taking of *excessive* interest. But this is not the meaning of the original Hebrew word, and the American Standard Version correctly translates the word by our word "interest." The taking of interest is consistently condemned in the Old Testament.[8] The only exception is the passage in Deuteronomy 23:20 in which the Hebrew is permitted to lend to the foreigner upon interest but not to his brother Hebrew. There is a vast difference between modern society in which capital is productive and

---

[7] Micah 2:2. (American Standard Version. Italics ours.)

[8] See Exodus 22:25; Leviticus 25:36; 36:37; Deuteronomy 23:19, 20; Psalm 15:5; Proverbs 28:8; Ezekiel 18:8-17; 22:12.

the simple society of the Hebrews in which loans were not usually made for productive enterprises. It is hard to see how modern society could function at all without the recognition of the right of a man to receive interest on his investments. But it is interesting to notice that the Marxian criticism of a capitalistic society considers the taking of interest a social sin and insists that no man has a right to receive that for which he has not labored. The implications for our life today of the Old Testament prohibition of the taking of interest need to be thought out afresh in the light of the criticisms which socialists are making of modern society.

The Law of the First Fruits
The Redemption of the First-Born

The laws of the Hebrews were so designed that the individual was forced constantly to acknowledge the divine ownership of all wealth. In the law of the first fruits, the Hebrew was required to bring to the Lord the first fruits of the harvest. In this way God was constantly recognized as the giver of the harvest.[9] The law of the first-born emphasized the same truth in the realm of man and beast. The Hebrews were required to redeem the first-born of both man and beast.[10] Through this law, God was acknowledged as the source of all life and there was set up in Israel a permanent memorial of the time when the first-born in Israel were redeemed from the angel of death. This law was still in force when Jesus was born, and one of the first acts of Joseph and Mary after the birth of Jesus was to present Him at the Temple in the rite of the redemption of the first-born.[11]

There is no reference to these laws in Paul's teachings concerning Christian stewardship. In part, they were designed to function when Israel was an independent nation. They could not be applied in detail in the world in which Paul lived. But the ideas which found expression in these laws were the common heritage of Judaism. They must have furnished a part of the background of Paul's thinking on the subject.

The Law of the Tithe

When we think of stewardship in the Old Testament, we must consider the laws we have mentioned. But the central thought of

---

[9] Exodus 23:16-19.
[10] Exodus 13:11-15.
[11] Luke 2:22-24.

the Old Testament concerning stewardship is found in the law of the tithe. As the tithe is constantly emphasized in Christian teaching concerning stewardship, it deserves special emphasis in a study of the Old Testament background of Paul's thought. The existence of the tithe as a proportion set aside as holy unto the Lord is revealed in Genesis. Abraham pays tithes unto Melchizedek, the king of Salem, as a priest of the most high God.[12] Jacob recognizes the existence of the law of the tithe as he makes his vow at Bethel. The law is found at various places in the Mosaic legislation. In Leviticus we read, "All of the tithe of the land, whether of the seed of the land, or of the fruit of the tree, is the Lord's: it is holy unto the Lord . . . . And concerning the tithe of the herd, or of the flock, even of whatsoever passeth under the rod, the tenth shall be holy unto the Lord."[13] In Numbers we read, "And the Lord spake unto Aaron, Thou shalt have no inheritance in their land, neither shalt thou have any part among them: I am thy part and thine inheritance among the children of Israel. And, behold, I have given the children of Levi all the tenth in Israel for an inheritance, for their service which they serve, even the service of the tabernacle of the congregation."[14]

The law of the tithe is reaffirmed in the strongest terms in Malachi, the last of the prophets. Malachi says, "Will a man rob God? Yet ye have robbed me. But ye say, Wherein have we robbed thee? In tithes and offerings. Ye are cursed with a curse: for ye have robbed me, even this whole nation. Bring ye all the tithes into the storehouse, that there may be meat in mine house, and prove me now herewith, saith the Lord of hosts, if I will not open you the windows of heaven, and pour you out a blessing, that there shall not be room enough to receive it."[15] This is the passage which serves as the basis of most of the sermons concerning tithing.

Religious Values in Tithing

As men have searched the Word of God for some principle to guide them in determining how much they ought to give to God, they have naturally turned to the Old Testament law of the tithe. Tithing has been preached as the solution of all the problems of

---

[12] Genesis 14:18-20.
[13] Leviticus 27:30, 32.
[14] Numbers 18:20, 21.
[15] Malachi 3:8-10.

Christian giving. There are very definite religious values in tithing. When we tell a man to give the tithe of his income to the Lord, we tell him something that is definite and concrete. The actual working out of the tithe may involve a good many complications, but the general principle is one that can be stated simply. The tithe is honoring to God because in tithing God's portion is taken out first. In the handling of his income, the wise man puts first things first. The money that is necessary for rent, food, clothing, etc., should be set aside before it is decided whether or not there is money for the luxuries of life. Unless a man has some systematic plan of giving he is apt to meet first all of the other demands that come to him, and give to the work of the Lord out of the remainder of his check. But if the gift to the support of the work of the church comes after all the other obligations are met, it is equivalent to saying that the support of the work of the Lord is not very important. Men honor God when they take out God's portion in the beginning.

The payment of the tithe comes also to men as a definite reminder of God's ownership and man's stewardship. An ownership which is not acknowledged is soon forgotten. But when men pay regularly a definite proportion of their income to the support of the work of God's Kingdom, they are constantly reminded of the fact that all that they have comes from God.

There is a distinct value also in the idea of a separated portion which is administered for God. The man who sets aside a definite portion of his income in a separated fund becomes an administrator of this fund for God. It is his responsibility to give his money in such a way that it shall be used wisely in the work of the Kingdom. In doing this, he must consider the various calls which come to him and decide between them. But these calls do not compete so much against his own selfishness as they compete against each other.

The Tithe in the New Testament

For the reasons we have given, and for many others, the revival of an emphasis on tithing has marked a distinct advance in the promotion of stewardship in the church. But it would be a great mistake for Christian leaders to think that they can solve the problems of Christian stewardship today simply by an intensified emphasis on tithing. Christian stewardship must go much deeper and have a broader basis than the Old Testament law of the tithe.

It must be admitted that the argument for the tithe in the New Testament is very weak. Jesus has a great many profound things to say about stewardship. But Jesus never mentions the tithe in His discussions of the attitude of a man toward his possessions. In fact, Jesus mentions the tithe only twice. In the parable of the Pharisee and the publican, Jesus makes the Pharisee say, "I give tithes of all that I possess."[16] And in the denunciation of the Pharisees, Jesus says, "Woe unto you, scribes and Pharisees, hypocrites! for ye pay tithe of mint and anise and cummin, and have omitted the weightier matters of the law, judgment, mercy, and faith: these ought ye to have done, and not to leave the other undone."[17] The question of the tithe is not really under discussion at all in this verse. Jesus is accusing the Pharisees of too much concern for trivial things and too little concern for the things that are really vital. The tithing of mint, and anise, and cummin is mentioned as an illustration of the concern of the Pharisees for the application of the law in its minute and unimportant details. And this concern of the Pharisees for trivial details stands out in sharp contrast with the way in which they have left undone the weightier matters of the law, which Christ defines as judgment, mercy, and faith. When Jesus says, "These ought ye to have done," He is referring to the demand of the law for justice, mercy, and faith. And His words "and not to leave the other undone" can hardly be made to mean more than the statement of Jesus that the concern with the minute details of the law such as the tithing of mint, anise, and cummin is not condemned by Him if it is not separated from a vital concern with the performance of the great moral obligations set forth in the law. When we view this casual reference to the tithe by Jesus in the midst of a passage which centers in His stern denunciation of the legalism of the Pharisees, we cannot feel that this passage can be properly interpreted as expressing either the approval or the disapproval by Jesus of the tithe as a principle of Christian giving.

There is no reference at all to the law of the tithe in the writings of Paul. The tithe is referred to in the letter to the Hebrews. But few, if any, scholars hold today to Paul's authorship of the book of Hebrews. And the references to the tithe in the seventh chapter of Hebrews are part of the larger argument for the pre-eminence of Christ. They have no relation to the question of stewardship in the

[16] Luke 18:12.
[17] Matthew 23:23.

early church. In I Corinthians the sixteenth chapter, verse 2, Paul summarizes the directions he gave in the churches for the taking of the collection for the saints. In this connection he says that each Christian should give "as God hath prospered him." In this way Paul points out the obvious principle that our giving should be in proportion to our income. It is possible to say that in this verse Paul demands proportionate giving and then go on and read into the verse the proportion that we receive from the Old Testament and in this way to build up an argument for the tithe. But it is also obvious that in such an argument we are reading into Paul's writings more than he has said. The absence of any reference to the tithe in the writings of Paul is particularly interesting in the light of the number of passages in Paul's letters which deal directly or indirectly with the question of stewardship. In his appeal for the raising of the collection for the saints at Jerusalem, Paul moves through the whole range of the motives to which a man might appeal to stimulate Christian giving. But we have no record of his ever mentioning the tithe.

The Tithe and Christian Giving

The absence of any reaffirmation of the principle of the tithe in the New Testament does not decide the case either for or against the tithe as a broad principle of stewardship. But the New Testament point of view concerning stewardship does open the way for a number of criticisms of the way in which the tithe is often presented. In the first place, the church must be very careful in her preaching of the tithe to remember the difference between law and grace. Paul insisted that Christians were *not under law but under grace.* He sought to get away from an external code and to move in the inner realm of man's response to the grace of God in Christ. There is a grave danger that in the preaching of the tithe we shall fall into a type of legalism which is not essentially different from the Jewish legalism which Paul rebelled against. And it is worthy of notice that in both of the rather derogatory references to the tithe which are found in the teachings of Jesus, the sarcasm of Jesus is directed against the tithe as part of a formal observance of the Jewish law which was detached from any full surrender of the life to God. The demands made upon us by our response to the grace of God in Christ are not less searching than the demands made upon us by the call to obedience to the law of God. But the demands of grace move in a different realm from the demands of law.

In the second place, there is a danger that the emphasis on the tithe in the church will result in the Christian's feeling that in the payment of the tithe he has discharged in full the obligations of Christian stewardship. This objection is not inherent in the idea of the tithe. It can be met with the idea of tithes and *offerings*. In this case the offerings are assumed to stand for that which is given over and above the tithe. And the acknowledgment of God's peculiar claim on a tenth of our income is not inconsistent with the acknowledgment of our responsibility to God for the use of all our income. In actual practice, however, many Chrsitians are apt to feel that the tithe is the full measure of their response to the call of Christian stewardship. But from a Christian point of view it is obvious that if the tithe is the measure of the obligation of a man on a limited income with heavy responsibilities, the tithe is not the measure of the obligation of a man on a much larger income with comparatively few responsibilities. Every sound principle of taxation of income moves along the line of an increasing percentage in the higher brackets of taxable income. Man's response to that which God has done for him under the Christian dispensation is a matter of grace, not of law. But if that response is to be "as God hath prospered him" it should take a larger percentage of the income of the rich than of the income of the poor.

As the opposite side of this same principle, it is a mistake to so interpret the tithe as binding on the Christian conscience that the very poor who cannot pay it are guilty of sin in their failure to tithe. Every Christian should covet the privilege of doing something for the support of his church. And the most glorious Christian giving is that giving in which people in the midst of their poverty honor God by putting the demands of His Kingdom first. The real support of the church comes not from the large gifts of the rich, but from the small gifts of the poor. And many churches which hold the bulk of their membership among the very poor have gloriously demonstrated through tithing the capacity of the poor to support their church. But to interpret the tithe as an absolute law binding upon all Christians regardless of their income or their obligations is to move out of the realm of grace and to drop back to the realm of Jewish legalism.

In the third place, we must avoid in our preaching of the tithe the danger of pitching our program of stewardship on a plane that is not distinctively Christian. The argument for the tithe moves in the realm of God's ownership and man's stewardship. It touches certain broad principles of religion which are common to all who believe in God. It would be equally valid for the Jew, or the Unitarian, or the Mohammedan, or the Mormon. It could be put forward either by the liberals or by the fundamentalists. But Christian giving must flow from our understanding of that which God has done for us in Jesus Christ. It is fair to say that with most Christians the will to tithe has been born of the surrender of the soul to the infinite love of God which meets us in the death of Christ on the cross. The church has never promoted her program of stewardship merely upon the call to obedience to a law of the Old Testament. But the church today needs to realize afresh that a great program of Christian action must be squarely based on convictions that are distinctively Christian.

Stewardship in Paul Is Based on Christian Convictions

It is here that we come to the peculiar importance of the teachings of the Apostle Paul concerning Christian stewardship. Paul knows the meaning of the death of Christ. He knows the response which the Christian should make to the love of God in Christ which was revealed at Calvary. Paul moves in the light of the resurrection of Jesus Christ from the dead. He sees all of our earthly life as it is called in judgment by the revelation of the resurrection world of God. For this reason Paul has in a unique way the understanding of the true relation between the material and the spiritual. Paul is a member of a great Christian brotherhood. It is a brotherhood which is born of God's great redemptive act. It is composed of those unto whom God has given His Holy Spirit. And Paul has, in a sense which is unknown in the Old Testament, an understanding of the demands that are made upon us because of our place in the great fellowship of those who believe in Jesus Christ. Paul is engaged in the great missionary enterprise of winning the world for Christ. He is the leader of a crusading Christianity which has a mighty passion to win men to Christ. For this reason, Paul is able to give us a point of view concerning stewardship that is different from that which is found in the Old Testament. The church must undergird her program of Christian activity today with a program of Christian stewardship which will furnish an adequate basis of support for the great enterprises of the church. And when the church turns to the Word of God for the Biblical basis upon which her program of stewardship must rest, she will find that she must come to the letters of Paul for the great insights that are to guide and stimulate Christian giving in the modern world.

QUESTIONS ON CHAPTER I

1. Why is it important to prepare for a study of Paul's thought concerning Christian stewardship by a survey of the teachings of the Old Testament on this subject?

2. What reasons did the Hebrews give for their belief in the divine ownership of the land?

3. How did the Hebrews frame their laws to prevent the ownership of the land from becoming concentrated in the hands of a few large landowners?

4. How does the study of the story of Ahab and Naboth illustrate the way in which the right of a man to his inheritance was held sacred in Israel?

5. What is the value for us today of the ideas underlying the land laws of the Hebrews?

6. Define the law of the tithe as it is to be found in the Old Testament.

7. What positive religious values are to be found in the practice of tithing today?

8. Discuss the treatment of the tithe in the New Testament.

9. How do the New Testament insights concerning Christian giving deepen the practice of tithing?

10. Why does Paul have a point of view concerning Christian giving which is not fully shared by the writers of the Old Testament?

CHAPTER II

The Sharing of Wealth in the Early Church at Jerusalem

THE conversion of Paul did not take place until a number of years after the beginning of the church at Pentecost. In the years preceding the conversion of Paul, the church at Jerusalem had grown until it represented a mass movement within Judaism. And Paul did not begin to exercise a dominating influence on the development of Christianity immediately after his conversion. It was not until Paul returned from his first missionary tour to defy the Judaizers at Antioch and Jerusalem that Paul began to stand out as the founder of the Gentile church and the aggressive leader of the Christian movement. By this time the church had been established in Jerusalem, in Judea, in Samaria, and in Antioch. When Paul came to leadership, he found therefore an established church which had already developed something of a program of stewardship. The Pauline world church grew out of this church. In this sense, Paul built on foundations that had already been laid.

THE SHARING OF WEALTH FOLLOWING PENTECOST

It becomes necessary, therefore, as a basis of our study of stewardship in the churches that Paul established, for us to study the foundations which were laid in the church before Paul assumed leadership.[1] When we examine the life of the early church in Jerusalem from this point of view, we find that there was in this church at the very beginning a most interesting experiment in the sharing of wealth. And as this experiment has often been misinterpreted, it becomes necessary to try to ascertain as accurately as possible just what happened in the church at Jerusalem and to consider the bearing of

[1] As a foundation for our study of the stewardship message of Paul, the relation between the teachings of Jesus concerning stewardship and the teachings of Paul should also be considered. A discussion of this will be found in Appendix I.

this experience of the early Christians on the program of stewardship in the church today.

In the second chapter of Acts we are told, "And all that believed were together, and had all things common; and sold their possessions and goods, and parted them to all men, as every man had need."[2] We have here as one of the effects of the coming of the Spirit into the lives of this first group of believers a remarkable experience. A brotherhood is formed in Jerusalem in which the members hold all things common. We have the spectacle of men selling their possessions and sharing with their brothers in Christ in accordance as each man had need. We seem to realize at the beginning of Christianity the goal of a community in which wealth is divided in accordance with need. In the beginning, this sharing of wealth seems to be unplanned and spontaneous. The great experience of Pentecost created a brotherhood in which the rich were willing to share with the poor on the basis of need.

In the fourth chapter of Acts, we find another statement of the sharing of wealth which went on in the early church at Jerusalem. We read: "And the multitude of them that believed were of one heart and of one soul: neither said any of them that ought of the things which he possessed was his own; but they had all things common. And with great power gave the apostles witness of the resurrection of the Lord Jesus: and great grace was upon them all. Neither was there any among them that lacked: for as many as were possessors of lands or houses sold them, and brought the prices of the things that were sold, and laid them down at the apostles' feet: and distribution was made unto every man according as he had need . . ."[3] This is a beautiful passage which describes the life of the early church in the midst of that warm glow of spiritual fervor which was born at Pentecost. The multitude of those that believed were of *one heart* and of *one soul.* From the midst of this fellowship the apostles with great power gave the witness of the resurrection of the Lord Jesus. And Luke concludes this part of his picture by saying, "and great grace was upon them all." An emphasis on this part of this passage is essential to an understanding of the passage as a whole. The supreme interest of the writer of the passage is in the wonderful Christian fellowship that was achieved in this church. The sharing of wealth which he mentions is described because it is an

[2] Acts 2:44, 45.

[3] Acts 4:32-35.

expression of the new spirit of brotherhood which was realized in the first Christian church.

But the genuineness of the spiritual experience of these first Christians is revealed in part in the new attitude toward their possessions which these believers assume. In the yielding of themselves to Christ, the Christians make Christ the master of their possessions. They no longer assert that what they have is theirs to do with as they please. Some of those who had lands and houses sold them and brought the money to the apostles. In this way there was created a common fund from which distribution was made to every man according as he had need. For the time being, at least, poverty was abolished. There was not to be found among these Christians any man who lacked for the essentials of life.

The effect of the existence of this kind of fellowship in Jerusalem must have been profound. We are told that "with great power gave the apostles witness of the resurrection of the Lord Jesus." This is not surprising. The presence in Jerusalem of a fellowship such as that which is described in Acts would be at once a proof to all men that a mighty power was at work in the lives of these people. The way is prepared for belief in the witness of the church to the resurrection of her Lord when this witness comes from the midst of a transformed community.

The picture which we have of this church is a beautiful one, and we would not underestimate either its beauty or its power. At the same time, we must not place an interpretation on this story which is not supported by all the facts involved. An examination of the story will show that there never was a time when all of the Christians in Jerusalem had sold their homes to create a common fund for the support of the Christian community as a whole. In Acts 2:46, Luke says of the Christians that "breaking bread at home, they took their food with gladness and singleness of heart."[4] The expression, "breaking bread at home," may be interpreted to mean that while they gathered daily in the Temple they ate at home. More probably the expression refers to the Communion service. In this case, it would mean that while the Christians gathered together in the Temple for worship they went from house to house to observe the Lord's Supper. But in either case the expression is evidence that most of the Christians retained their homes. The probability is that even in the first enthusiasm of the birth of the church each man who was

[4] American Standard Version.

able to do so continued to provide for his own family in his own home. From the beginning, the distribution from the common fund was probably made only to those who were in need.

The Sin of Ananias and Sapphira

The story of Ananias and Sapphira brings out this truth. The first sin that appears within the fellowship of the New Testament church is in connection with the program of sharing of wealth that was carried on in the church. Barnabas had a piece of land and sold it and gave the money to the apostles. It is possible that Barnabas did this because he was aware of some particular case of need within the church. And we are not told that Barnabas sold everything he had. He did sell some land and he brought the money from the sale of the land and laid it at the apostles' feet. This act of Barnabas must have made a profound impression on the members of the Jerusalem church. Within every church there is a desire on the part of the members of the church to stand well with the other members. And evidently the deed of Barnabas made such an impression that Ananias and his wife desired to get the credit for a similar act. Incidentally, the effect of the act of Barnabas on the church at Jerusalem is part of the argument to show that there never was in this church the requirement that all the members of the church should sell their possessions and turn the money over to a common fund. If any such requirement as this had existed within the church at Jerusalem, the act of Barnabas would have passed almost unnoticed. It was because Barnabas did *more* than most of the members of the church had done that his generous deed called forth comment within the church.

Ananias and Sapphira were guilty of the sin of hypocrisy. They wished to appear better than they were. They wished to receive within the church the credit for a deed similar to that of Barnabas. For this reason Ananias and Sapphira sold a possession and gave part of the money over to the apostles. At the same time they pretended that they were turning all of the price of the land over to the apostles.

When Peter rebukes Ananias for this deed he says: "Whiles it remained, was it not thine own? and after it was sold, was it not in thine own power? why hast thou conceived this thing in thine heart? thou hast not lied unto men, but unto God."[5] The words of Peter

[5] Acts 5:4.

show that the right of private property was not called in question in the Jerusalem church. Ananias was a member of the church, but the land that he owned was regarded as his to do with as he saw fit. Of course as a Christian he would have to face the change in his attitude toward his possessions involved in his becoming a Christian. But he was not required to sell his land as a condition of being received into the Christian community. And when he had sold his land he was still free to dispose of the money he had received from the land as he saw fit. He could have given all of it, or part of it, or none of it to the church. The sin of Ananias was not the sin of giving a part of the price of his possession to the Lord. The heart of his sin was his desire to gain prestige in the church by getting credit for a more generous gift then he was willing to make. And the sin of hypocrisy involved, as it usually does, the sin of lying. But our peculiar interest in the story of Ananias at this time is in its revelation of the nature of the experiment in the sharing of wealth which we find in the Jerusalem church. And the story of Ananias and Sapphira conclusively proves that the early Christians never contemplated a sharing of wealth which meant that every Christian was expected to sell his possessions and turn the money into a common fund.

The Ordaining of Deacons

The first recorded sin in the early church came in connection with the creation of a common fund out of which the apostles were to minister to those in need. And the first division which arose to mar the fellowship of the same church came in connection with the distribution of this fund. A natural line of division in the Jerusalem church lay between the Grecians and the Hebrews. The Grecians were Greek-speaking Jews who had lived in various parts of the Roman Empire before coming to Jerusalem. The Grecians are not to be confused with the Greeks who represented, of course, the members of the great Greek race. The Grecians were Jews, but they were Jews who spoke the Greek language. When the term Hebrews is used in contrast to the Grecians, it describes the Jews who had always lived in the Holy Land. On the whole the Grecians were much more apt to be tolerant of foreign ideas than were the Hebrews. And the Grecians were the first to realize the universal implications of the Christian faith. Stephen, Philip, and Paul were all Grecians. The first division in the Jerusalem church came as the murmuring of the

Grecians against the Hebrews because their widows were neglected in the daily ministration.[6] The complaint of the Grecians shows that there was a daily ministration in the church at Jerusalem. This would mean that out of the common fund enough food would be bought to send a daily supply to those in need. But this complaint of the Grecians does not seem to indicate that the daily ministration was for the church as a whole. The supply of food that was sent out each day was for the *widows.* Others who were unable to care for themselves were doubtless included in this ministration. But the vast majority of the Christians must have continued to live normal lives in which each man who was able to do so provided in his own home for those who were dependent upon him.

The answer of the apostles to the murmuring of the Grecians brings out the difficulties which the apostles were beginning to experience in the administering of relief within the church. The twelve call together the multitude and say: "It is not reason that we should leave the word of God, and serve tables."[7] Perhaps the apostles reveal a little of spiritual pride in their unwillingness to be concerned with the details of the daily ministration. And as a matter of fact, with the exception of Peter and John none of the apostles are heard of any more, and Stephen and Philip, two of the deacons who are *appointed to serve tables,* become the leaders in an advancing Christianity. But the main point of the apostles is sound. Men who are called to positions of spiritual leadership cannot afford to allow all of their energies to be consumed in details that are more or less secular in nature.

The first deacons were those who were chosen and ordained by the apostles in the church at Jerusalem. They were appointed to relieve the apostles of the details of the daily ministration to the poor. This office was continued in the churches that Paul established. And in I Timothy, we find Paul laying down the qualifications of the deacon.[8] The office of the deacon is still perpetuated in many of the

---

[6] Acts 6:1.

[7] Acts 6:2.

[8] I Timothy 3:8-13.

In the reviews which I have received of my *Social Message of the Apostle Paul,* I have been criticized because I refer to the pastoral epistles, I and II Timothy and Titus, as Pauline, and because I use the book of Acts as one of the sources of our knowledge of Paul's thought. For a brief discussion of this see Appendix I. In this book the pastoral epistles will be referred to as Pauline without the raising of this point again, and the book of Acts will be used as a valid source for our study of the life and thought of Paul.

Protestant churches. And the task of the deacon is usually conceived in terms of relieving the pastor of the financial problems involved in the managing of the business affairs of the church.[9] In the beginning the office of the deacon was created in order that the deacons might have supervision of the administration of relief in the church. This particular function of the deacon has more or less been overlooked as the church in the modern world has ceased to assume any large responsibility for the administration of relief.

The Church Was Not Communistic

There was nothing in the sharing of wealth in the Jerusalem church which could be identified as communism in the sense in which the term communism is used in the modern world. The basic assumption of the understanding of society which prevails in modern communism is that the tools of production belong to the people as a whole. But the Christians at Jerusalem never made any effort at realizing a society in which there was a common ownership of the tools of production. Each man earned his money as best he could in the society in which he lived. All that these Christians did was to create a common fund from which distribution was made to those who were in need. Modern communism is interested primarily in the production and distribution of material goods. But the central interest of the Christians at Jerusalem was in religion rather than in economics. The sharing of wealth came as the expression of a brotherhood that was achieved on a religious basis. The sharing of wealth in modern communism is on the basis of force. In Russia, for example, the state has seized by force the tools of production and the communistic society is set up on the basis of compulsion. But the sharing of wealth that went on in the church at Jerusalem was on a voluntary basis. Behind the giving of these Christians there was the pressure of the whole Christian understanding of the brotherhood of man in Christ. But this pressure was a moral pressure exerted on the will and the final decision rested with each individual.

We must not make too much out of the example of the sharing of wealth in the church at Jerusalem. But at the same time we must not underestimate the importance of this story. These Christians

[9] The office of the deacon has been developed along these lines in the Presbyterian Church in the United States, popularly known as the Southern Presbyterian Church. A similar development has not taken place in the Presbyterian Church, U. S. A.

realized a brotherhood in Christ. It was a brotherhood in which, for a time at least, poverty was abolished. Those who had much shared with those who had little. And a world which had known very little of love or brotherhood was suddenly confronted with the spectacle of a brotherhood which went so deep that there was experienced on the basis of love a real sharing of wealth among the members of the church.

The Development in the Pauline Churches

The question at once arises as to the extent to which the pattern that was laid down at Jerusalem became typical of the other churches that were built in the New Testament period. This question is particularly important as we turn to a study of the churches as we see their life and work reflected in the Pauline Epistles.

When we judge the experiment at Jerusalem on the basis of the long view we must admit that it did not prove a permanent success. For a time poverty was abolished. But a little later we find that the Christians at Antioch are sending relief to the saints at Jerusalem.[10] And during the whole of his ministry among the Gentiles, Paul was constantly engaged in raising funds for the church at Jerusalem.[11] It is possible that too free an attitude in the beginning toward the giving of help to those in need was responsible in part for the creation in Jerusalem of a situation in which some of the people were constantly in need of help.

After the dispersal of the church in the persecution that followed the death of Stephen, it became impossible for all the Christians to unite in the creation of a common fund from which a daily ministration was made to all who were in need. But the fundamental idea of the church as a brotherhood in which those who had much shared with those who had less, remained characteristic of the church in the whole New Testament period. John writes: "But whoso hath this world's good and seeth his brother have need, and shutteth up his bowels of compassion from him, how dwelleth the love of God in him?"[12] John suggests that the readiness of a man who has this world's goods to share with his brother in Christ who is in need is one of the tests of the presence of the love of God in a human life.

---

[10] Acts 11:27-30.

[11] Acts 24:17; Romans 15:25; I Corinthians 16:3; II Corinthians, chapters 8 and 9.

[12] I John 3:17.

And John is very much concerned that Christian love shall express itself in actual deeds of ministry to those who need help.[13]

And there is abundant evidence that the churches which Paul founded were brotherhoods in which the rich shared with the poor in a ministry to human need.[14] The details of the way in which this sharing of wealth was worked out probably varied widely in different churches. And Paul at times had to lay down regulations to prevent the abuse of the administration of relief in the church. He himself usually set the example of earning his own living. And he instructed the Thessalonians that "if any would not work, neither should he eat"; he urged the busybodies "that with quietness they work, and eat their own bread."[15] He wrote Timothy, "If any provide not for his own, and specially for those of his own house, he hath denied the faith, and is worse than an infidel."[16] He warned Timothy against receiving on the relief roll of the church the younger widows.[17] He insisted that if possible each believing Christian should care for the widows connected with his family, that the church might be relieved of this burden and might be able more adequately to relieve those who were widows indeed.[18] All of these injunctions against the abuse of relief in the church are, however, a part of our evidence that the churches Paul founded were actively and systematically engaged in administering relief to those of their members who were in need. And, as we shall see in later chapters, Paul extended this idea until he envisioned the whole Christian society as so organized that the need of one section of the church would be supplied by the abundance of another section.[19]

A Brotherhood Based on Love

When we have put together all of our various bits of information, we find that the general pattern of the New Testament church was not essentially different from the pattern of the church in the modern world. In the beginning there was in the church at Jerusalem a readiness to hold all things common which did not prove perma-

[13] I John 3:18.
[14] Galatians 2:10; Romans 12:13.
[15] II Thessalonians 3:10, 12.
[16] I Timothy 5:8.
[17] I Timothy 5:9.
[18] I Timothy 5:16.
[19] II Corinthians 9:13.

nently feasible even in the church at Jerusalem and was never extended to the churches scattered over the Roman Empire as a whole. And as we have seen, this sharing in the church at Jerusalem never went so deep as might seem to be indicated by one or two statements when these statements are viewed apart from the picture which we get from the study of the book of Acts as a whole. The New Testament Christians had to enter the economic order of their day and earn their living as best they could. And each man was expected to do all that he could to provide for himself and his dependents. But the church did constitute a brotherhood in which on a voluntary basis the Christians united to take care of those of their fellowship who were in need. In this way the Christians stood together against the extremes of economic need. And they gave to the pagan world a remarkable demonstration of a brotherhood based on love.

But while the general pattern of the church that is reflected in the pages of the New Testament was not essentially different from the pattern of the church today, it is true that the churches of the New Testament period achieved a brotherhood in Christ which went much deeper in its sharing of wealth than most churches do today. In many cases, the church today has almost ceased to function at all in the field of relief. In the modern world, the state, operating with funds raised by taxation, has almost supplanted the church as the agency for the administration of relief. The problems of relief involved in the period of depression, for example, were too vast to be handled through the churches or through private charity, and in recent years we have seen a wide extension of the administration of relief through state-supported agencies. The proper co-ordination of the work of state and church in the field of relief will always remain a difficult problem. But the church of Jesus Christ should never become a brotherhood in which men remain indifferent to the material needs of those who are their brothers in Christ. In this respect, as in many others, the New Testament church has set for us a pattern which should remain both the inspiration and the goal of the church in every age.

QUESTIONS ON CHAPTER II

1. Show that the church had established a program of stewardship before the time of Paul's assumption of leadership in the church.

2. Describe the sharing of wealth that took place among the Christians immediately after Pentecost.

3. Show that the sharing of wealth among the Christians in the first church at Jerusalem did not involve the demand that every Christian as a condition of membership in the church should give all that he had to the common fund.

   (a) How does the story of the gift of Barnabas bear on this point?

   (b) How does the story of Ananias and Sapphira show that the Christians were permitted to retain their property?

4. What was the nature of the dispute between the Grecians and the Hebrews as to the treatment accorded their widows?

5. How does this story show that even in the early church at Jerusalem distribution was made only to those in need?

6. What was the function of the deacon in the early church?

7. Contrast the sharing of wealth that took place at Jerusalem with the sharing of wealth in modern communism.

8. To what extent was the experiment in the sharing of wealth in the church at Jerusalem duplicated in the Pauline churches?

9. To what extent was the experiment in the sharing of wealth in the church at Jerusalem modified in the Pauline churches?

10. What is the permanent message to the church today that comes from this experiment in the sharing of wealth which marked the first church at Jerusalem?

CHAPTER III

The Christian Attitude Toward Work

MAN MUST WORK

THERE was work in the Garden of Eden. Man was placed in the Garden of Eden "to dress it and to keep it."[1] And part of the curse that falls on man when sin enters the picture is that for him work becomes toil. To the sinning man and woman it was spoken, "In the sweat of thy face shalt thou eat bread."[2] In the picture of the man and woman who must eat their bread in the sweat of their brow we have set forth the conditions under which all of human life must be lived. The earth is the nourisher of life. God has placed man upon the earth and God has placed in the earth all of the things that are necessary for the support of the life of man. But the earth does not bring forth of itself the things that man needs. If left alone the earth will bring forth thorns and thistles. Man must cultivate the earth if he expects to get the bread which he must eat. There are a few spots upon our earth in which a limited number of people might live on a very low plane of human existence without working. But in most parts of the earth man must toil for his food, his clothing, his shelter. Man eats his bread in the sweat of his brow, and if any man does not eat his bread in the sweat of his own brow, he is eating it in the sweat of someone else's brow.

MAN MUST SUBDUE THE EARTH

Alongside of the fact that man in his earthly existence must eat his bread in the sweat of his brow, we should place the primal command to man to *subdue* the earth. The history of the human race is, in part, the history of man's effort to master his environment. Man has asserted his mastery over the beasts of the field. The animals that could not be tamed have been conquered, and the animals that were useful to man have been domesticated and forced to serve the purpose of man. Gradually man has learned the secrets of the

[1] Genesis 2:15.
[2] Genesis 3:19.

earth. He has learned to so understand the forces of the natural world that he has forced the world of nature to serve his purpose. In recent years, the progress of man in subduing his earth has been amazing. Man can send his voice around the earth. He can send his ships beneath the surface of the sea. He can fly over the roof of his world. He has dug into the earth and has forced the coal, and the oil, and the gas to serve his purpose.

And the end of these things has not yet been reached. Amazing possibilities for the control of nature for the good of man open before our generation. Man has reached the stage in human history when through the combination of science and industry it is possible to produce enough to give to every man an abundance of food and enough of the products of industry to give him the material basis for a satisfying life.

All Men Should Work

Because the earth does not bring forth of itself, man must work. And no able-bodied man has a right to a life that does not share something of the burden of toil that the human race must bear as the earth is forced to yield her increase. Any man who lives without working is in one way or another a pensioner on the labors of others. We would acknowledge at once that there are many kinds of work. Man must labor with his hands that man may live. Man must labor with his brain that life may be worth while. But no matter how rich he may be, the man who sits back and lives off the wealth which other people create, while hc contributes nothing either by hand or brain to the work of mankind, is a pensioner on society as a whole.

Paul as a Laborer

Jesus knew the meaning of toil. Before He entered upon His public ministry, He worked for many years in the carpenter shop at Nazareth. He took his part in the task of molding the fruit of the earth to the service of mankind. And Saul of Tarsus, like every other Jewish boy, was taught a trade. His trade was tentmaking. Probably young Saul of Tarsus never expected to earn his bread by the making of tents. But in his life as a Christian missionary his knowledge of this trade proved at times most helpful, as he was forced to provide for his own support during the time that he was establishing himself in a city. For example, when Paul first came to Corinth he stayed with Aquila and Priscilla and worked with them because they were tentmakers.[3] And in his letters as a whole Paul is constantly referring to the fact that he at times earned his living by working with his hands. We can almost see him as he holds up his worn hands to the elders of Ephesus and says, "Ye yourselves know, that *these hands* have ministered unto my necessities, and to them that were with me. I have shewed you all things, how that so labouring ye ought to support the weak."[4] And in his letter to the Ephesians he advises them to labor, working with *their hands*.[5] He writes to the Corinthians: "Even unto this present hour we . . . have no certain dwellingplace; and labour, working with *our own hands*."[6] And he tells the Thessalonians to attend to their own business and to work with *their own hands* as he had commanded them.[7]

The Dignity of Manual Labor

On the basis of the references we have given, we can say that Paul has a profound respect for the dignity of manual labor. In the upper classes of society there has been found at times a tendency to depreciate the dignity of labor. This sentiment has found expression, for example, in the saying, "A gentleman does not work with his hands." Such a sentiment would find little support in the writings of Paul. Any kind of work that is honest is honorable. Of course, it is not a wise economy of man's effort for highly skilled labor to be employed in unskilled work. And it would be absurd for men who are highly trained for the professions to give the major portion of their time to a type of manual labor which could be done just as well by untrained labor. Paul was able to make his living making tents. He was not ashamed at times to follow this trade as a means of making a living. But we can be thankful that the major effort of Paul's life did not go into the making of tents. The world would have been infinitely the poorer if Paul had been too busy making tents to have time to write the letter to the Romans.

The Necessity of Mental Labor

Those who labor with heart and brain should never depreciate the labor of those who make their living working with their hands. At the

---

[3] Acts 18:1-3.
[4] Acts 20:34, 35.
[5] Ephesians 4:28.
[6] I Corinthians 4:11, 12.
[7] I Thessalonians 4:11.

same time those who literally make their living in the sweat of their brow should not depreciate the toil of those who labor in other ways. The teacher who stands all day in the classroom may know a type of nerve strain that is unknown to the man who tills the soil. Those who carry large responsibilities in business and politics often carry these responsibilities at a cost to themselves that is very heavy. And the minister who bears the spiritual responsibility of the shepherding of a congregation may know an exhaustion at the end of a day's work which goes far beyond the tired feeling of the man who works with his hands. But while each man must work in his own way, every man who is able to do so should know the meaning of work.

Reasons for Work

1. Fear of Hunger

In urging his converts to work, Paul gives a number of reasons for the necessity of work. When we put these together we have a fair summary of the reasons why men must work. He tells the Thessalonians, "If any would not work, neither should he eat."[8] The fear of hunger will always be one of the great driving forces for the motivation of human labor. Men must work because men must eat. Men cannot live without food. And every man must work because it is through his work that he earns the money that buys the food to support his life and the lives of those who are dependent on him. Paul moves on the same general plane of thought when he tells the Thessalonians to work in order that they "may have lack of nothing."[9] Men must work because it is only through their labor that they will be able to get the things they need. Man needs food. But man needs much more than food. Men face the elemental needs of clothing and shelter. These things are necessary if life is to continue. And any man who is to move in the life of the modern world faces a large range of needs which go beyond the bare essentials of life and at the same time are necessary if life is to be lived on a high plane. There is the need for books, the need for transportation, the need for money for the education of children, or for medical expenses. And for the great majority of people the only way that they can attain independence in life is by exchanging their labor for the money which will buy the things they need. The mention of these things seems to move on a

---

[8] II Thessalonians 3:10.
[9] I Thessalonians 4:12.

very simple plane of thought. But in touching these motives Paul is moving on the plane of the actual living of many people. Men must work because if they do not work they cannot eat. Men must work because they have need of many things that they cannot get without working for them.

2. *To Be Honest*

Paul tells the Thessalonians that they are to work that they "may walk honestly toward them that are without."[10] And he writes to the Ephesians, "Let him that stole steal no more: but rather let him labour, working with his hands the thing which is good."[11] Behind both of these commands there is the understanding that for most men it is difficult to live honestly without working. Underlying most of the dishonesty in the world there is the desire of men to get something they have not worked for. This may be seen in its simplest form as men prefer stealing the corn another man has worked to raise rather than being willing to do the work necessary to the raising of their own corn. In the more complex structure of modern society the presence of this motive may not be so obvious. But when we carefully analyze the situation we find that usually the motive of trying to get something for nothing underlies in one way or another most of the "get rich quick" schemes through which men hope to grow rich without having at the same time any concern to render to society a service that is proportionate in value to the money they hope to receive. But men assume an essentially dishonest attitude to life when they are always trying to get something for nothing. Behind all of the various forms of gambling which are found in modern life there is the same desire to get something for nothing. The desire of people to get something they have not worked for is one of the most effective motives to which men may appeal. But it is not a moral motive. The fabric of modern society is corrupted because of the attempts of men to live without working, to seize for themselves a wealth they have done nothing to create.

3. *Working the Thing That Is Good*

Paul tells the Ephesians that they must labor, "working . . . the thing which is good."[12] In his emphasis on "the thing which is good,"

---

[10] I Thessalonians 4:12.
[11] Ephesians 4:28.
[12] Ephesians 4:28.

Paul strikes another note that should be characteristic of the labor of the Christian. Every Christian should seek to work at something that is worth while. He should seek through his labor to create something that is good. A Christian has no right in his work to be associated with something that is evil. There are some occupations that are closely related to the underworld. No Christian has a right to earn his living through the illegal handling of alcohol or through running a gambling joint. The Christian must constantly scrutinize the sources of his wealth to be sure that he is working the thing that is good. And the Christian should seek to get into some work which ministers to a real human need. It is in this spirit that Jeremiah writes: "Woe unto him that buildeth his house by unrighteousness, and his chambers by wrong; that useth his neighbour's service without wages, and giveth him not for his work."[13]

4. To Be Able to Help Others

Paul strikes a higher note in his argument for the necessity of work when he says that a man should labor, "that he may have to give to him that needeth."[14] This is a much more definitely Christian motive than the motives we have considered so far. Regardless of whether or not a man is a Christian, there is in him the fear of hunger, the desire for independence, and usually the concern to live honestly and to work at something worth while. But the Christian has a deeper motive for working. In his heart there is a desire to have something to share with those who are in need. And unless a man produces more than he needs for himself he will have nothing to share with others. It is in this connection that Paul preserves for us in his speech to the leaders of Ephesus a saying of Jesus that has not been preserved for us in any of the Gospels. He closes his speech by saying: "I have shewed you all things, how that so labouring ye ought to support the weak, and to remember the words of the Lord Jesus, how he said, It is more blessed to give than to receive."[15] It is strange that these words of Jesus were not preserved for us in any of the Gospels. The natural tendency of the human heart would be for a man to think that it was a more blessed experience to receive than to give. But Jesus taught men that there was greater joy in giving than in receiving. Paul had found this to be true in his own

---

[13] Jeremiah 22:13.
[14] Ephesians 4:28.
[15] Acts 20:35.

experience. At times he received gifts. He knew the joy of being the object of the love and care of his people. But Paul knew also the deeper joy of being able (because through his own labor he had earned more than he needed for his support) to support the weak and to minister to human need. To the man who has a Christian attitude toward life this is one of the most important reasons for working. Unless we create by our labor more than we need for ourselves we shall never have the wealth with which to minister to the needs of others. When we look at this truth on a grander scale we can realize that unless a people creates by its labor more than it consumes it will be impossible to accumulate the wealth necessary for the large works of charity. Unless we produce more than we consume there will never be wealth to build orphanages, or to endow schools, or to build churches, or to support missionaries. In this sense a man's money is his stored-up labor. It is the medium of exchange through which he gives himself.

To any man who sees life as a Christian it is a great source of satisfaction to be able to use his wealth to minister to human need. And when men through the honest fruits of their toil have accumulated large wealth there opens up to them an amazing range of opportunities for making this wealth count in helping others. Such a man can have the joy of making it possible for the boy who is brilliant but poor to receive an education. He can prepare the way for the medical missionary to minister to suffering humanity in a distant land. He can build churches in needy communities. And such a man is certain to learn the meaning of the words of the Lord Jesus, "It is more blessed to give than to receive." But men do not have to wait until they grow rich to know the meaning of this saying of Jesus. In fact, those who do not begin to experience the joy of giving while they have little to give from are not apt to know much about giving when wealth has increased. Every Christian should have as one of the reasons for working the desire to have something to give to those who are in need.

Paul's Advice to the Workers

In Ephesians and Colossians, Paul deals with the attitude a man should take toward his work. His advice is set in the framework of the institution of slavery but the truths which underlie his words are applicable to any order of society. We will consider first his word to the workers and then his word to the employers of labor. In Colossians, he writes: "Servants, obey in all things your masters according to the flesh; not with eyeservice, as menpleasers; but in singleness of heart, fearing God: and whatsoever ye do, do it heartily, as to the Lord, and not unto men; knowing that of the Lord ye shall receive the reward of the inheritance: for ye serve the Lord Christ. But he that doeth wrong shall receive for the wrong which he hath done: and there is no respect of persons."[16] The companion passage to this in Ephesians is: "Servants, be obedient to them that are your masters according to the flesh, with fear and trembling, in singleness of your heart, as unto Christ; not with eyeservice, as menpleasers; but as the servants of Christ, doing the will of God from the heart; with good will doing service, as to the Lord, and not to men: knowing that whatsoever good thing any man doeth, the same shall he receive of the Lord, whether he be bond or free."[17]

1. *Not in Eyeservice*

Paul condemns the attitude toward work which he describes as "eyeservice." Every employer of labor is familiar with this kind of labor. There are workmen who are concerned to do just as little as they can to hold their jobs. These are the servants who work when you watch them and do not work when they are sure that no one can check up on whether or not they are working. Such an attitude toward work is fundamentally dishonest. If a working man sells ten hours of his day to an employer it is a matter of common honesty for him to try during that time to seek faithfully to do the work he is hired to do. A Christian should never be guilty of the kind of work that can be called "eyeservice."

2. *Not as Menpleasers*

Paul says also that the Christian should not work as "menpleasers." The thought here is close to the thought contained in the word "eyeservice." But it is possible for a man to do his work in a way that is satisfactory to his immediate superiors and at the same time do a cheap and shoddy piece of work. The pupil in the school, for example, may work with "eyeservice." He may be concerned to do just as little as the teacher will let him get by with. But the pupil needs a deeper basis for study than the desire to please the teacher.

---

[16] Colossians 3:22-25.
[17] Ephesians 6:5-8.

Many teachers are very slack in their requirements. The pupil needs to learn thoroughness and faithfulness in work regardless of the demands that the teacher makes upon him. And the worker in industry needs to get an attitude toward his job that goes beyond the demands made upon him by his immediate superiors. Those who work merely with "eyeservice, as menpleasers" will never go very far in the mastery of their jobs.

3. Fearing God

Paul supplies a deeper motivation for a right attitude toward our work when he says that Christians should do their work in singleness of heart, fearing God, and that whatsoever they do, they should do it heartily, as to the Lord, and not unto men. In this way Paul would lift all service to man to the plane of service to God. The Christian knows that the Christ is by his side when he works. The Christian should face every task that is laid upon him as the work which it is Christ's will for him to do that day. And the Christ demands that he put the best that he has into every job he undertakes. The eye of Christ sees every flaw in our work. There is nothing that we can hide from Him. He is aware of the mistakes that we can cover up from the eyes of men. He knows when we have done less than our best. He demands that we shall always do our work heartily as unto Him and not unto men.

If men would catch this attitude toward work which Paul sets forth it would transform the way in which many a job is done. The teacher who is not a Christian may teach merely as a means of earning her living. She may have no interest in her work beyond that of pleasing the principal under whom she works. But the Christian teacher should know that in her attitude toward her work she is responsible to the Christ whom she has made Lord of her life. The work she has to do is the task He has willed for her. And she should seek to discharge her duty in a way that will be pleasing to her Lord. The doctor who is not a Christian may assume an attitude toward his profession that is coldly commercial. He may be in the practice of medicine without interest, either in people or in medicine. And if this is his attitude, his practice of medicine may be filled with many things that are not entirely ethical. But the doctor who is a Christian should remember that the Christ is always by his side as he practices his profession. If he does this he will seek to do his work in a way that is pleasing to Christ. This point of view, if fully understood, will make impossible the careless and indifferent practice of medicine. The politician may be tempted to do the thing that is popular. He is naturally very much concerned to be a pleaser of men. But the politician who is a Christian will know that his responsibility to his Lord runs deeper than his responsibility to his constituents. The purifying effect of this principle on politics is obvious.

Men reveal their character more by the way in which they work than by the way in which they pray. The real fiber of a man's character is often determined by his attitude toward his job. The child who slights his work in school is beginning to develop a wrong attitude toward his job. And the child who consistently slights his work will find that he is undermining the whole basis of character. Every man must give an account unto God for the way in which he does his work.

4. The Worker's Reward

Every Christian should do his work as unto the Lord. And Paul is certain that the Christian who does his work in this way will not lose his reward. The Christian is to do his work as unto the Lord because he knows that of the Lord he will receive his reward. Over all men as they work there stands the Christ. He is the Lord of the universe and He will so order His universe that men reap the consequences of their deeds. The man who cheats as he does his work may avoid the judgment of men, but the Christ who controls our universe will bring it to pass that the wrong which he has done will return unto him again. And the same Christ will see to it that no faithful service remains ultimately unrewarded. In this way, Paul sets all men before the judgment bar of God as they do their work. Even within all the injustice of our present world order, it is usually true that faithful work brings in time its recognition and its reward. And it is equally true over a long period of time that the man who slights his work will usually reap the consequences of his laziness and his indifference. But Paul is not thinking here in terms of the approval or disapproval of men. And he is not thinking of the compensations which men can give or fail to give. He has his eyes fixed on Jesus who is the Christ, the risen Lord, the Lord of history. In Him, there is an evenhanded justice which knows no respect of persons. He requires of every man that in accordance with his ability he should do the task that is set before him. And He will be the ultimate judge of every man's work. The difference between the Christian and the non-Christian as each man faces his work is that the Christian must do his work as one who labors in the presence of the living Christ. And this means that the Christian must understand his earthly task in a way that is not possible to the man who has refused to acknowledge God in Christ.

Paul's Advice to Employers

1. *A Master in Heaven*

Paul would apply to the employers of labor the same fundamental ideas that he applies to the work of the laboring man. He writes, "Masters, give unto your servants that which is just and equal; knowing that ye also have a Master in heaven."[18] And he writes in Ephesians, "Ye masters, do the same things unto them, forbearing threatening: knowing that your Master also is in heaven; neither is there respect of persons with him."[19] Every man who uses the labor of others must remember that over him there is a Master in heaven. In his handling of his labor, every man must remember that he must give an account unto the Lord Jesus for the way he deals with those who work for him. And as Paul thinks of the masters, he repeats his statement that there is no respect of persons with God. The employer and the employee stand before the same God. Each man in his own situation is responsible to the God who has revealed Himself in Jesus Christ. No man ever grows so rich or so powerful that he ceases to stand before the judgment bar of God.

2. *Rendering That Which Is Just and Equal*

And because every employer must face his Master in heaven, he must forbear threatening and he must render unto his workers that which is just and equal. We cannot attempt to say in advance just what is just and equal in any given situation. This must be determined in each individual case in the light of the whole social situation. And if there is a real will on the part of both employer and employee to determine the treatment that is just and equal, it should not be impossible in any given situation to reach an agreement that is fair both to the worker and the employer. The Christian employer differs from the non-Christian employer in that the Christian must at all times so live that he can give an account of himself to the

---

18 Colossians 4:1.

19 Ephesians 6:9.

risen Christ. And if the Christian employer knows that as an employer of labor he must stand in this relation to God, he will find that his whole attitude toward labor is determined by the fact that he is a Christian.

3. Brothers in Christ

Finally, Paul would remind both master and slave, both employer and employee, that they are brothers in Christ. He told Philemon to receive Onesimus as a brother in Christ. He told the Colossians that in Christ Jesus there was no such thing as bond or free. In our world, he would certainly add that in Christ Jesus the barrier between employer and employee is transcended. One of the great tasks of the church in the modern world is to build a fellowship in which the deep divisions of modern society are transcended. Over against the divisions between the workers and their employers there should be set the great Christian conception of the unity of all men in Christ. The church must build in the modern world a fellowship in which employer and employee, rich and poor, capitalist and proletariat, stand together before the God who has come to men in Jesus Christ.

QUESTIONS ON CHAPTER III

1. What is the meaning of Genesis 3:19—"In the sweat of thy face shalt thou eat bread"?

2. Trace the way in which man has fulfilled the command to "subdue" the earth.

3. How did Jesus bear His share of the world's toil?

4. What trade was Paul taught as a part of his training as a Jewish boy?

5. How did Paul find his knowledge of his trade useful in his missionary labors?

6. How does Paul exalt the dignity of manual labor?

7. What reasons for work does Paul appeal to when urging on his converts the necessity of work?

8. How does Paul describe the way in which a Christian should do his work?

9. What reward for faithful work does Paul promise to Christian workers?

10. Why does Paul say that masters should render unto their servants that which is just and equal?

11. What is the meaning both for employers and employees of the Christian principle that with God there is no respect of persons?

12. How does Paul visualize the chasm between employer and employee as bridged in Christ?

CHAPTER IV

The Stewardship of All of Life

Deepening the Basis of Stewardship

WITHIN the Christian church as a whole, the word stewardship is an unpopular word. In the minds of most people the word calls up associations that are not altogether pleasant. This is because the people of the church have come to think of stewardship largely in terms of the raising of money. The emphasis on stewardship in the church calendar is usually associated with the putting over of the church budget. And there is a danger that the people of the churches will come to feel that the program of stewardship in the church is a thinly veiled attempt to separate them from their money. For this reason, most congregations have developed as a sort of protective measure an effective sales resistance to the whole stewardship program.

But as a matter of fact the emphasis on the stewardship of possessions is only a part of the call of the church to the stewardship of all of life. And the challenge of the church to the dedication of possessions cannot be understood unless it is seen against the larger background of our whole attitude toward life.

In the original meaning of the word, a steward was "an officer or employee in a large family, or on a large estate, to manage the domestic concerns, supervise servants, collect rents or income, keep accounts, etc."[1] In the ancient world, the steward was thought of as a man who handled things that were not his own. The steward handled the revenues of a large estate, but he was supposed to handle them in the interest of the owner of the estate. And the steward was expected to be ready at any time to give an account of his stewardship. The basic idea involved in the word stewardship is therefore adequate to describe the attitude which a man should take toward himself and his possessions as he realizes he must give an account unto God. God is the owner. Man is the steward. God has trusted us with certain material goods which He lets us administer for a time. But

[1] Webster's Collegiate Dictionary.

no man is the absolute owner of that which he has. Every man must give unto God an account of his stewardship.

The danger in the preaching of stewardship as we have outlined it is that stewardship will be presented in terms that are not distinctively Christian. We have already pointed out the similar danger in an exclusive emphasis on tithing.[2] But this danger is apt to be present in the whole stewardship program of the church. The danger is that in talking about stewardship, the church will think in broad terms of God as owner and man as steward without seeing the unique relationship in which man is set to God in the Christian understanding of redemption. If our thinking concerning stewardship moves merely in the broad realm of a natural theology common to all believers in theism, we shall not have laid the basis for the continuing support of the activities of the Christian church. It is our purpose in this chapter to try to see the distinctively Christian understanding of life as it bears on the whole question of stewardship.

To Be Pleasing to Christ

Paul has given us in the fifth chapter of II Corinthians a superb statement, his understanding of the meaning of the Christian life. In attempting to explain to his critics the driving power of his life, Paul says, "We make it our aim . . . to be well-pleasing unto him [Christ]."[3] This then was the aim of Paul's life. His whole purpose in life was to so live that he would be pleasing unto Christ. In the next verse, he extends this idea to include the idea of a final judgment in which all men stand before the judgment seat of Christ. He says, "We must all appear before the judgment seat of Christ; that every one may receive the things done in his body, according to that he hath done, whether it be good or bad."[4] There is a deep seriousness which comes over life when men realize that they are moving on to a judgment in which they must give an account unto Christ of the deeds done in the body. Of course, Paul does not think exclusively in terms of an ultimate judgment in which all men must stand before God. It is his aim, whether in the body, or out of the body, to be pleasing to Christ. He sees every man as set during the whole of his existence in the relation of one who must give an account of his every act unto Christ.

---

[2] Chapter I, pages 24, 25.

[3] II Corinthians 5:9. (American Standard Version.)

[4] II Corinthians 5:10.

The Love of Christ Constraineth

We draw nearer to the heart of our question when we ask why Paul sees all men in this relation. Why does Paul feel that he *must* so live that he is pleasing to Christ? What is the driving power of the Christian's life? Paul answers these questions as he says, "The love of Christ constraineth us." By "the love of Christ" he does not mean his love for Christ. It is true that as Paul understands the love of Christ he responds in love to the divine love. As John writes, "We love, because he first loved us."[5] Man's love springs from the fountain of the divine love. But the driving power of Paul's life is to be found in his understanding of the love of Christ for him. It is because Paul has been laid hold of by Christ's great love that he feels he must carry on in his God-given ministry.

One Died for All

In the verse that follows, Paul makes it very clear that the love of Christ is revealed to him in the death of Christ on the cross. He says, "The love of Christ constraineth us; *because we thus judge,* that one died for all, therefore all died; and he died for all, that they that live should no longer live unto themselves, but unto him who for their sakes died and rose again."[6] Paul says that the love of Christ is a constraining power in his life because of his understanding of the death of Christ. At many times there has been a tendency within the Christian church for men to feel that the theory which a man has of the Atonement is unimportant. And there is some justification for this feeling when men deal in hairsplitting differences concerning minor points of theology. But the way in which a man understands the death of Christ is not unimportant. The way in which men respond to the love of God in Christ is inevitably rooted in their understanding of what God has done for them in Christ. In this sense a man's theory of the Atonement is vital to his understanding of the meaning of the redemption wrought out in Christ.

It is therefore with an understanding of the importance of our study to the whole conception of Christian stewardship that we seek to understand the meaning of the death of Christ to Paul. In giving his theory of the Atonement Paul says: "The love of Christ constraineth us; because we thus judge, that *one died for all.*"[7] He

---

[5] I John 4:19. (American Standard Version.)
[6] II Corinthians 5:14, 15. (American Standard Version. Italics ours.)
[7] II Corinthians 5:14. (American Standard Version. Italics ours.)

further defines what he means by saying that "one died for all" by saying, "God was in Christ reconciling the world unto himself, not reckoning unto them their trespasses."[8] In verse 18 he says, "All things are of *God, who reconciled us to himself through Christ.*"[9] And in verse 21 he says, "Him who knew no sin he made to be sin on our behalf."[10] In these verses Paul sets forth a clearly defined understanding of the death of Christ. He says that *one died for all;* i.e., that the death of One was in place of the death which all others would have been required to give if the death of Christ had not taken place. This is a part of the great Christian conviction in which a man expresses his faith by saying, "Christ died for me. He died in my place." If the Christian is asked why it was necessary for Christ to die for him, he must answer that Christ died to reconcile us to God. In this there is involved the whole understanding of the barrier between God and man which is created by man's sin. Paul would have utterly no patience with that type of theology in which "a God without wrath, saves man without sin, by a Christ without a cross."[11] He has a tremendous consciousness of the wrath of God, a wrath which must be expressed against human sin. When he thinks in terms of man's salvation he knows that man needs salvation from the wrath of God. He cries out in Romans, "The wrath of God is revealed from heaven against all ungodliness and unrighteousness of men."[12] And if asked to explain what happened on the cross, he would say that on the cross, the sinless One became sin for us.

No man can understand perfectly the meaning of the cross of Christ. There is here an element of truth which always escapes us. Here, as in all of man's higher thinking, we must seek to lay hold of truth in the full realization that none of us is able to comprehend fully the meaning of the great redemption that was wrought out on Calvary. Man never betrays more fully his misunderstanding of the cross of Christ than when he approaches this great mystery of the Christian faith without the humility and the sense of awe and wonder which should be characteristic of man in the presence of the revelation of the divine. But the great fundamentals of the Christian understanding of the death of Christ can be expressed in terms that any man can understand. The death of Christ was vicarious. He died

[8] II Corinthians 5:19. (American Standard Version.)
[9] American Standard Version. (Italics ours.)
[10] American Standard Version.
[11] John Mackay in *Preface to Theology.*
[12] Romans 1:18.

for us. The death of Christ was substitutionary. He died in our place. In His death, Jesus Christ became sin for us. God was in Christ reconciling the world to Himself. The barrier between God and man was removed by the death of Christ.

The Christian Must Live for Christ

Our fundamental interest in this study is not, however, so much in Paul's theory of the death of Christ—as important as that is—as it is in his understanding of the effect of the death of Christ on the believer. He writes, "We thus judge, that one died for all, *therefore all died*."[13] We cannot be perfectly sure of Paul's meaning here, but if we interpret the verse against other passages in which Paul works out a similar idea, we can say that the believer who receives the salvation wrought out for him in Christ passes through an experience in which he dies to one life that he may live unto another. The Christian dies unto sin and lives unto God. Paul understands the purpose of the death of Christ as involving a fundamental change in the attitude of the believer toward life. He says, "He [Christ] died for all, that they that live should no longer live unto themselves, but unto him who for their sakes died and rose again."[14] When a man accepts the death of Christ as God's atonement for his sin, there should be a fundamental shift in his attitude toward life. The Christian no longer lives unto himself. He must live unto Him who for his sake died and rose again. When men yield themselves to the love of God in Christ they find that they have experienced a shift in the center of their being. In Paul's words, "If any man is in Christ, he is a new creature: the old things are passed away; behold, they are become new."[15]

Christ Has Redeemed Us

When Paul cries out to the Christian, "Ye are Christ's; and Christ is God's,"[16] he is not thinking in broad terms of God as creator and man as steward. He is not moving on the plane of natural religion. Instead he is thinking in definite terms of the way in which men have been laid hold of by the redemptive activity of God. The implication of this truth for Christian preaching is obvious. It is absurd to call men to the practice of Christian stewardship until we have first

[13] II Corinthians 5:14. (American Standard Version. Italics ours.)
[14] II Corinthians 5:15. (American Standard Version.)
[15] II Corinthians 5:17. (American Standard Version.)
[16] I Corinthians 3:23.

called them to the surrender of life to God in Christ that is demanded in the Christian gospel. In this sense, a message of evangelism is essential to any message of Christian stewardship. And this message of evangelism must be expressed in terms of the historic Christian understanding of the meaning and purpose of the death of Christ.

Christian Stewardship Roots in Christian Conviction

Wherever Christians have given largely and sacrificially it has been because their giving was rooted in an understanding of the meaning of the death of Christ which is similar to that set forth by Paul. The springs of giving have always dried up when men have sought to explain away the great revelation of God on Calvary in terms that blurred the distinction between Christianity and other religions. The writer remembers in this connection a comment made by his instructor in Theology, Dr. Thomas Cary Johnson. The remark was made in connection with the discussion of the loss of Andover when this school was merged with the School of Theology at Harvard. Dr. Johnson said, "The Unitarians have never been particularly liberal in the supporting of their institutions. God hasn't done very much for man on Unitarian principles." And the history of the Christian church as a whole bears out Dr. Johnson's comment. One of the most remarkable features of Protestant Christianity in the last hundred years is the great program of missionary expansion through which Christianity was carried from Europe and America and planted in germ at least in almost every section of the inhabited world. But the missionary passion of Christianity was rooted in clearly defined convictions concerning God and man. Its driving power was the passion to bring men to God in Christ as the only way of salvation for man in this world or in the next. The great missionary program of the last hundred years was conceived and sustained by a Christianity that was rooted in the great Christian convictions that have always been the springs of Christian action.

Christian stewardship in its deepest sense is impossible apart from the surrender of man to God in Christ. But when Paul cries out, "Ye are Christ's; and Christ is God's," he goes on to say, "Let a man so account of us, as of ministers of Christ, and stewards of the mysteries of God. Here, moreover, it is required in stewards that a man be found faithful."[17] The Christian is Christ's. He must think of himself

[17] I Corinthians 4:1, 2. (American Standard Version.)

as Christ's man, as Christ's servant. The Christian is a steward of the great revelation which God has given in Christ. The stewardship of the gospel is committed unto him. He shares with other Christians the responsibility of giving the gospel to others. It is required of stewards that a man be found faithful. The Christian must so live that he discharges faithfully the obligations that are laid upon him as a servant of Christ and a steward of the mysteries of God.

Stewardship of Time

One way in which the Christian will discharge his responsibility as a steward is through the rendering of an account to God of the way in which he uses his time. All of us have the same amount of time. We vary greatly in the amount of money which we have at our disposal, but each of us has twenty-four hours a day, seven days in the week, and fifty-two weeks in the year. All men have the same amount of time. The difference is in the way in which they use it. Only a small fraction of the members of the Christian community will ever be able to give their full time to Christian service. And no minister will ever be entirely free from worldly cares and avocations. In this situation, it is the responsibility of every Christian to acknowledge Christ as the Lord of his time and to think through his time to decide how he may best use it for the glory of God. If a man is in a position in which he must earn a living for himself and for those dependent on him, he will naturally have to set aside a large portion of his time for the proper attention to his business. We do not increase in our capacity to serve God through the neglect of the duties that are laid upon us in the earning of a living.

But if Christ is the Lord of our time, we will not become so absorbed in the making of a living that we have no time for the making of a life. In the world today much is being said about priorities. The principle that lies behind priority is that when we have a limited amount of anything we must so distribute it that the most important things come first. A Christian should apply the principle of priority to his time. He should so discipline himself that in the use of his time first things come first. Every man who has the will to do so can arrange his time in such a way that he has some place in his life for private and for public worship. This does not mean that the Christian should spend all of his spare time attending religious meetings. Each Christian must decide for himself whether his time is best used in attending some religious service, or in the reading of a book, or in the cultivation of the life of his family, or in many of the other worth-while ways in which a man may use his time. There should be in every man's life some time for rest and recreation. In the long run we will serve God best as we learn to rest in order that we may work better.

In many cases the need of the church for members who will render an adequate stewardship of their time to God runs deeper than the need of the church for stewardship of possessions. In every church, only a limited number of people are willing to give in any large way of their time to the service of Christ. Sunday-school classes are not taught, or are poorly taught, because Christians cannot be found who are willing to give the necessary time to the study of the lesson. The work of evangelism falters in the church because Christians are unwilling to give to soul-winning the time that it requires. The services of the church are poorly attended because Christians are unwilling to so organize their time that they can have time for the regular attendance at public worship. If we are Christ's and Christ is God's, it follows that Christ is the Lord of our time. He asks us to organize our time with the understanding that we are always responsible to Him for the way in which we use our time. The consistent application of this principle by the members of any church would work far-reaching changes in the life of the church.

Stewardship of Abilities

Any true understanding of stewardship must also involve the stewardship of abilities. If a man has yielded his life to Jesus Christ, it follows that the abilities that he has should be laid on the altar of the service of God. Men vary very widely in their abilities. There are some who have one talent and there are some who have ten talents. God does not demand of any man the rendering of an account for the abilities he does not have. But Jesus does lay down the principle that what God expects of us is in proportion to that which He has given us. He says, "For unto whomsoever much is given, of him shall be much required: and to whom men have committed much, of him they will ask the more."[18]

The proper stewardship of abilities is necessary to the effective functioning of the Christian community. Those who have gifts in music can serve God through their music. Those who have the capac-

---

[18] Luke 12:48.

ity for teaching can serve through their teaching. The man who has a brilliant mind has a responsibility to God for the use of his mind in the service of God. Those who have natural gifts of leadership can express these gifts through leadership in the various activities of the church and the Kingdom.

The larger the powers a man has the greater the temptation to misuse or to selfishly use of these powers. Our temptations come to us through our powers and range around our powers. One of the tragedies of the life of the church is that many men of large ability have failed to understand their stewardship as a Christian in terms of the dedication of their powers to the service of God. All too often the work of the church is done by men of few talents because those of many talents are unwilling to dedicate their talents to the service of God. The ability that goes undiscovered and unused in the average church constitutes a colossal waste of power. As a means of stimulating men to dedicate their abilities to the Lord, the church should constantly remind men that each man is expected to render a stewardship that is in proportion to the talents he has received. The man with large gifts must render a service that is in proportion to his gifts. The ten-talent man has not discharged his responsibility to God when he is content to render the same kind of service that the one-talent man can render. God has given to us a diversity of gifts, and He requires that each man shall render his stewardship of the talents he has received.

Stewardship of Possessions

The stewardship of possessions must be seen against the background of man's response to the love of God in Christ. It roots in that larger surrender of his whole personality to God which a man makes when he acknowledges Jesus Christ as Lord and Master of his life. The stewardship of possessions must be seen in the setting of the stewardship of all of life. The proper stewardship of time and ability is just as important as the stewardship of possessions. But when this larger background of stewardship has been thoroughly understood, it inevitably follows that the lordship of Christ in a man's life must express itself in the use which he makes of his possessions.

A man may give his possessions without giving himself. Men who have grown rich in this world's goods may in a limited way give of their possessions to the support of the Kingdom of God without ever yielding themselves in love and devotion to Jesus Christ. Men may give to causes in which they are not interested because of social pressure or to maintain their standing in the community. Of course, this kind of indifferent giving would never permanently support the great enterprises of the Kingdom. The Christian program of action must be supported by those whose giving is rooted in Christian convictions. But it is true that a man in a limited way may separate himself from his check.

A man may give of his wealth without giving himself, but no man can give himself to God without letting the surrender of himself carry with it the lordship of Christ over his possessions. In this sense, a man's use of his possessions is often the revelation of the extent to which he has dedicated his life. If Christ is Lord of our lives He must also become the Lord of our possessions.

If a man is to be Christian in his use of his possessions, he must be ready to give an account to Christ of all of his spending. It is only when he can best serve the Kingdom of God by spending his money on himself, that he has a right to spend on himself. This means that every Christian should think through with Christ the whole question of his spending. The application of this principle does not mean that a Christian has no right to spend on himself and on those who are dependent on him. Very often the money that a man spends on his own education becomes his wisest investment in Christian service. Every Christian faces the elemental responsibility of providing for himself and for those who are dependent on him. In the same way, there is nothing wrong in the way in which a man feels the necessity of providing during the days of his capacity to earn for the days of sickness and old age which may lie ahead. The application of the same principle does not mean that the life of the Christian should be devoid of all the comforts and conveniences of life. It is through the conveniences of modern life that men are being set free from the drudgery of life in the past and are being enabled to give themselves more freely to the larger purposes of living. And there is nothing unchristian in a man's investment of a portion of his income in productive enterprises. His capacity to give in the future will be related to the soundness of the financial policy which he sets in the present for himself and his family. No one should interpret the lordship of Christ over his possessions in terms which deprive human life of the higher cultural values. There is a place in the Christian scheme of things for music, art, and literature. And in most families a reasonable expenditure for amusements has a proper place in the building of a balanced life.

But the lordship of Christ over our possessions does mean that every expenditure for ourselves must be considered in the light of the relation of this expenditure to the whole work of the Kingdom. And this principle should curb among Christians all needless extravagance and display in the spending of money. If a man has passed through the experience in which he has ceased to live for himself and has come to live for the Christ who died for him, he must express this surrender of life through using his possessions in a way that is pleasing to Christ. And if a man shuts off from the lordship of Christ the vast area of his life which deals with the getting and spending of money, it follows inevitably that the lordship of Christ in that life is not yet complete. If this great area of his life remains among the things he has not yielded to God, it means that Christ is shut out of one of the most important parts of his life. Such a man cannot hope to grow in grace or in spiritual power. Jesus Himself has asked the great question, "If therefore ye have not been faithful in the unrighteous mammon, who will commit to your trust the true riches?"[19] In the lives of many Christians, all real progress in spiritual life waits upon the willingness of that Christian to make Christ the Lord of his possessions and to render unto God a faithful stewardship of the things that God has given him.

---

[19] Luke 16:11.

QUESTIONS ON CHAPTER IV

1. Why is the preaching of stewardship unpopular in the church?

2. What is the original meaning of the word "steward"?

3. Point out the danger in presenting our teaching concerning stewardship in terms that are not distinctively Christian.

4. How does Paul define the aim of his life?

5. Why does Paul say that the Christian should seek to be pleasing to Christ?

6. What does Paul say is the constraining power of his life?

7. Where does Paul find the revelation of the love of Christ?

8. Why is our understanding of the meaning of the death of Christ important as the basis of Christian stewardship?

9. What does Paul understand to be the true response of the Christian to God's great redemptive act in Jesus Christ?

10. How should Christian stewardship express itself in a stewardship of time?

11. How should Christian stewardship express itself in a dedication of our abilities to God?

12. Why is it that the complete surrender of the soul to Christ must inevitably express itself in the stewardship of possessions?

13. How is it that the failure to render a true stewardship of our possessions blocks our spiritual growth?

CHAPTER V

Fellowship in Ministering to the Saints

THE VARIOUS OFFERINGS TAKEN FOR THE CHRISTIANS AT JERUSALEM

ONE of the dominating passions of Paul's life was that the brotherhood of men in Christ should express itself through voluntary offerings in which the Christians ministered to their brothers in Christ who were in need. As an expression of this spirit, Paul at various times played a leading part in the raising among the Gentile churches of an offering for the suffering saints at Jerusalem. During his ministry at Antioch he was sent along with Barnabas to Jerusalem as the bearer of such an offering.[1] He brought a similar offering when he made his last visit to Jerusalem.[2] When he reached his agreement with James, Peter, and John at the Council of Jerusalem, they requested that the Gentiles should continue to remember the poor, and Paul adds, "the same which I also was forward to do."[3]

THE PURPOSE OF THESE OFFERINGS

Paul had a double purpose in his emphasis on the offerings to be raised among the Gentiles for the relief of the saints at Jerusalem. He was concerned, as always, with the ministry to the poor. He was interested also in the offering from the Gentiles to the saints at Jerusalem because he felt that this offering would be the means of binding together the Gentile and Jewish wings of the church. He wanted to bear the offering from the Gentiles to the Jews as the visible expression of the unity of the church.

Scattered throughout Paul's letters there are a number of references to the raising of this offering. When these references are studied carefully they give us a very clear idea as to the way in which Paul went about the raising of the offering among the Gentile churches.

---

[1] Acts 11:27-30 and 12:25.
[2] Acts 24:17.
[3] Galatians 2:10.

They reveal the motives to which he appealed. They give us his understanding of the attitude which a Christian should take to his possessions. And they set for us the plane upon which a program of Christian stewardship should be pitched today.

Returning Carnal Things for Spiritual

Paul's letter to the Romans was written from Corinth about 57 A.D. In this letter Paul writes: "But now I go unto Jerusalem to minister unto the saints. For it hath pleased them of Macedonia and Achaia to make a certain contribution for the poor saints which are at Jerusalem. It hath pleased them verily; and their debtors they are. For if the Gentiles have been partakers of their spiritual things, their duty is also to minister unto them in carnal things."[4] A little later in the same chapter, Paul asks the Romans to pray with him "that I may be delivered from them that do not believe in Judaea; and that my service which I have for Jerusalem may be accepted of the saints."[5] In this passage we see Paul's determination to bear this offering to Jerusalem in spite of his keen consciousness of the danger to himself involved in it. That this danger was very real is shown by the treatment which Paul did receive when he arrived at Jerusalem.[6] The same passage reveals Paul's consciousness of the obligation resting upon the Gentile churches to minister to the Christians in need at Jerusalem. Christianity had spread from Jerusalem as a center. The priceless privileges which the Gentiles had received in Christ had come to them through the Jews. And Paul feels that as the Gentiles have received this ministry in spiritual things they are under an obligation to express their appreciation through a ministry in carnal things.

Instructions Concerning the Collection for the Saints

1. *Taken on Sunday*

In his letters to the Corinthians, Paul reveals the large part which he took in arousing the Gentile Christians to the discharge of their obligation. In the sixteenth chapter of I Corinthians, Paul passes from the great chapter on the resurrection to a discussion of the orders he has given for the taking of the collection for the saints.

---

[4] Romans 15:25-27.
[5] Romans 15:31.
[6] Acts 21:26-40.

The rules that he lays down for the taking of the offering at Corinth are the same as those he had given to the churches of Galatia. They must have represented therefore his customary treatment of the subject in the churches to which he ministered. He writes: "Upon the first day of the week let every one of you lay by him in store, as God hath prospered him, that there be no gatherings when I come."[7] There is some question as to why Paul specified the first day of the week as the day upon which the collection was to be taken. But probably the reason for this was that the first day of the week, or the Lord's Day, was already being chosen as the day of the week for the Christians to assemble themselves for worship. In this respect, therefore, Paul anticipates the way in which the churches today take their offerings on the Lord's Day in connection with the gathering of the people for public worship.

2. Taken on a Weekly Basis

It is clear also that Paul instructed his churches to take their offerings on a weekly basis. This does not mean that the example set by Paul is binding upon the churches today. There will always be some who prefer to give to the church on a monthly or quarterly basis. But the majority of those who support the work of the church will find that they can carry their pledge more easily if it is paid on a weekly basis. And most churches operate on a budget that falls due at least once a month. It is most important for the work of the church that the income of the church should be on a sustained basis that is spread over the year as a whole. In the long run, this is just as true of the gifts to the benevolences of the church as it is of the gifts to current expenses where the monthly basis of the obligations of the church is more easily apparent. An additional argument for the giving to the church on a weekly basis is to be found in the way in which most churches build the offering into their worship service. The members of the churches are better able to participate in the weekly offering as an act of worship if their giving to the church is on a weekly basis.

3. As God Has Prospered

Paul says that each Christian should give as God has prospered him. We have referred to this clause in our discussion of the tithe. Without raising again the issues considered there we can say that a

[7] I Corinthians 16:2.

man's responsibility to give to the causes of the Kingdom is always related to the way in which God has prospered him. As Paul says in II Corinthians, "If there be first a willing mind, it is accepted according to that a man hath, and not according to that he hath not."[8] The man who has little from which to give need never feel that he is being disloyal to his Lord if his gift is small. On the other hand, the man whom God has prospered has a responsibility in giving that increases with his prosperity.

4. Avoiding High-Pressure Collections at the End

Paul insists on regular collections on a weekly basis in order that there may be no gatherings when he comes. If giving is carried on through a regular and systematic laying aside of a portion of our income as it comes in, we shall not find it necessary to make high-pressure collections at the last moment.

Paul's Care in the Handling of the Offerings

1. Through Men Chosen by the Churches

In his comments in the sixteenth chapter of I Corinthians, Paul introduces us to the extreme care with which he handled the offerings that were taken in the churches. He says: "And when I come, whomsoever ye shall approve by your letters, them will I send to bring your liberality unto Jerusalem. And if it be meet that I go also, they shall go with me."[9] These verses show us that Paul insisted that the churches should appoint men to travel with him and deliver in the name of the churches the offering to the church at Jerusalem. He returns to this idea in II Corinthians. In the seventeenth verse of the eighth chapter, he refers to his sending of Titus to the church at Corinth. He adds, "And we have sent with him the brother whose praise is in the gospel throughout all the churches."[10] We do not know who the brother was whose praise was in the gospel throughout all the churches. Some commentators have suggested that Paul in this verse was probably referring to Luke. But regardless of who the man was, Paul describes him as a man in whom all the churches have confidence. The reason for this is given in the next verse, in which Paul reminds the Corinthians that this man who has

[8] II Corinthians 8:12.
[9] I Corinthians 16:3, 4.
[10] II Corinthians 8:18.

the confidence of all the churches has been chosen by the churches to administer the offering which Paul is promoting. Paul writes: "And not that only, but who was also chosen of the churches to travel with us with this grace which is administered by us to the glory of the same Lord, and declaration of your ready mind."[11]

It would seem that Paul was overcautious in this matter. Those who knew Paul could hardly have doubted his integrity in the handling of the funds entrusted to his keeping. But Paul had many enemies. His enemies were always trying to find some point at which they could criticize him. And when we consider the large sums of money that probably passed through his hands we can see the wisdom of his determination not to lay himself open to criticism in his handling of the gifts of the churches.

2. Providing for Things Honest in the Sight of God and Man

In the next two verses, he states the principle upon which he worked. He says, "Avoiding this, that no man should blame us in this abundance which is administered by us: providing for honest things, not only in the sight of the Lord, but also in the sight of men."[12] He expresses the goal of all administrators of church funds when he says that this offering is to be administered to the glory of the Lord. But he shows great wisdom when he provides for honest things not only in the sight of the Lord, but also in the sight of men. These two principles need to be held in balance. If we think only of providing for things honest in the sight of men, we shall miss the deep principle that men must administer all of the finances of the church as men who stand in the sight of the Lord. But if we fail to take thought for things honest in the sight of men, we make it possible for men to lose confidence in the way in which the finances of the church are handled.

As an application of the principle which Paul has laid down we can say that all of the financial dealings of the church should be kept open to the public. Accounts should be kept accurately. The books of the treasurers should be audited regularly, and the whole financial life of the church should be carried on in a businesslike manner.

We face a larger application of this principle when we say that those who give the money that goes to the support of our churches

---

[11] II Corinthians 8:19.
[12] II Corinthians 8:20, 21.

have a right to insist that this money shall be spent to the glory of God. The springs of giving are certain to dry up when men begin to be doubtful about the way in which their money is used. Those who administer the funds of the churches are faced with a high and holy stewardship. They should not spend on themselves any more than is necessary to equip themselves for their task. They should avoid all extravagance in the conduct of the business of the church. They should at all times provide for things honest in the sight of God and men.

Paul's Promotion of the Offering

As we study Paul's references to the offering that he was taking in the churches for the saints at Jerusalem, we can see that Paul did not fail to prepare the churches for the offering. He seems to have gathered around him a group of men who were active in arousing the church to the need of the saints at Jerusalem. In I Corinthians 16:15, 16, he writes: "I beseech you, brethren, (ye know the house of Stephanas, that it is the firstfruits of Achaia, and that they have addicted themselves to the ministry of the saints,) that ye submit yourselves unto such, and to every one that helpeth with us, and laboureth." From this it would seem that Stephanas and his family had taken a special interest in the effort to minister to the saints. Paul commends Stephanas and urges the churches to receive him and to be in subjection to him. In II Corinthians, the eighth chapter, he says that he has requested Titus, "that as he had begun, so he would also finish in you the same grace also."[13] Evidently Titus has already visited Corinth to arouse the people to the need for this offering. And now Paul is sending him back to Corinth to complete the work he has begun. He is sending with Titus "the brother . . . whose praise is in the gospel throughout all the churches," whoever this person may be. And we can be sure that this man was expected not only to handle the money but also to arouse the people.

The principle upon which Paul works here is absolutely essential to the promotion of the work of the church. When the Gentile Christians saw the need for this offering as Paul saw it they gave to it in a way that called forth the highest of praise from the great apostle. But they would never have done this if Paul and his helpers had not taken the initiative in arousing the church. John writes,

---

[13] II Corinthians 8:6.

"Whoso hath this world's good, and seeth his brother have need, and shutteth up his bowels of compassion from him, how dwelleth the love of God in him?"[14] The thing that John wishes to condemn is the tendency on the part of a Christian to shut up his bowels of compassion when he sees that his brother has need. But Christians in one part of the world will not be aware of the need of their brothers in another part of the world unless someone who knows the situation presents the need to them in a way that makes them see it. In the mind of Paul, there was much more than a ministry to human need involved in this offering. He saw the church about to split into a Jewish church and a Gentile church. He knew that each section of the church needed the other section. He knew that a divided Christendom would not be able to stand in the difficult days ahead. This offering was to him a piece of well-planned ecclesiastical strategy. Through it he was laying hands on both the Gentile and the Jewish sections of the church and binding them into a unity that could not be broken. But the great mass of the Gentile Christians would not see this great issue unless Paul made them see it. It was his responsibility under God to arouse the churches of Macedonia, Achaia, and Galatia to their day of opportunity.

On the basis of Paul's example we ought to say a word of commendation of those men who have the responsibility for arousing the church to the tasks that God has set for her in our generation. The great mass of the members of the church are not able to keep in touch with the opportunities that arise as the church confronts her world task. Many of them have few contacts with those who are actually at work on the mission fields. All too often they know little or nothing about the great educational task of the church. And the particular emergencies that arise over the church as a whole do not usually fall within the horizon of their knowledge. All honor to those servants of God who see the need and then give themselves to the task of arousing the church to their vision of the world's need.

The Basis of Paul's Appeal

While Paul used Timothy, Titus, Stephanus, and others to help arouse the church, he himself was probably the master hand in the awakening of the church. The eighth and ninth chapters of II Corinthians are a skillfully framed appeal designed to arouse the

---

[14] I John 3:17.

church at Corinth. The significance of these chapters is that in them Paul roots his appeal in the heart of the Christian faith. The cause for which he appealed grew out of a temporary emergency caused by a famine in Judea. But the way in which Paul relates his appeal to the meaning of Christianity is for us a superb example of the way in which other appeals can be related to the great heritage which all Christians have in Christ.

1. Proving the Genuineness of Your Love

Paul begins by describing for the Corinthians the grace of God which had fallen on the churches of Macedonia. As he tells his story we realize that while he is describing what has happened in Macedonia he is also describing what he wants to happen at Corinth. Paul is not above the appeal in a mild way to the competitive motive. He has boasted to the church in Macedonia that the church in Achaia was ready a year ago.[15] But he is very careful to prepare the Corinthians for his coming to them lest he should be ashamed in his boasting. He has praised the Corinthians to the Macedonians, and he praises the Macedonians to the Corinthians. While the competitive motive is always an effective motive, it should not be overworked in appeals for giving. Christians must have a deeper basis for their giving than the appeal to give because someone else has given. But Paul makes an important point when he tells the Corinthians that he will prove by the earnestness of others the sincerity also of their love. Among the Macedonian Christians the love of the Gentiles for their brothers at Jerusalem has issued in a remarkable offering of their wealth. And the genuineness of the love for their brothers in Christ which exists among the Christians at Corinth will be revealed by their response to the same offering. If the love of the Christians at Corinth had not gone deep enough to translate itself into action, there would have existed in Paul's mind a real question as to whether the love of the Christians at Corinth was genuine. The real interest that the members of a congregation have in a cause is usually revealed in the way in which they give to it.

2. The Grace of Giving

Paul reminds the Corinthians of the *grace* of God bestowed on the churches of Macedonia. By this he means that the spirit of giving which has appeared in the churches of Macedonia is to be explained

---

[15] II Corinthians 9:2.

only as a grace which God has bestowed on His church. He understands that this thing has happened in Macedonia because God is behind it. Paul has been used of God to arouse the church, but he has been little more than an instrument in the hands of God. The thing that is happening in Macedonia roots in the Spirit of God moving in the hearts of the people.

3. A Fruit of the Spirit

The grace of giving Paul considers to be a fruit of the Spirit which must be listed along with the other graces that have appeared in such abundance in the church at Corinth. He writes to the Corinthians, "Therefore, as ye abound in every thing, in faith, and utterance, and knowledge, and in all diligence, and in your love to us, see that ye abound in this grace also."[16] One of the fruits of the Spirit in the life of a church is the growth of the church in the grace of giving. And the failure of a church to grow in the grace of giving may be a symptom of the presence in the life of the church of things that block the work of the Spirit.

4. Giving Out of Their Poverty

Paul says that the giving of the Macedonians was in the midst of their deep poverty. He himself is amazed at their giving. He feels that they have given to their power and beyond their power. Indeed, the abundant flowering of the grace of liberality in the midst of the poverty of the external circumstances of the Macedonian Christians presents to Paul a strange study in contrasts. The beauty of the spirit of the Christians overshadows the drabness of their surroundings.

5. Fellowship in Ministering to the Saints

Once they have been aroused to the situation, the Macedonian Christians beg Paul and his companions to take upon themselves "the fellowship in the ministering to the saints." In this phrase they show that they catch the real meaning of Paul's purpose. At the heart of the Apostle Paul there was a great compassion for his suffering brothers at Jerusalem. The Macedonian Christians did not know the Christians at Jerusalem. They did know Paul. They felt the compassion of his great heart. They wanted to enter into fellowship with him in his work of ministering to the saints. Through their

---

[16] II Corinthians 8:7.

offering they could have fellowship with Paul in the work that was so close to his heart.

6. *The Gift of Themselves*

Paul says that the Macedonian Christians "first gave their own selves to the Lord, and unto us by the will of God."[17] In their giving we have an example of the true order in Christian giving. They did not give their gift apart from themselves. First of all, they yielded themselves to God in Christ. They placed themselves in harmony with the will of God. In his demand on the Macedonian Christians, Paul put first things first. He led men to Christ, and he had the joy of seeing those whom he had led to Christ as they expressed their new life in Christ by a new readiness to give to their brothers in need.

7. *The Example of Christ*

As Paul seeks to stimulate the giving of the Corinthians, he holds before them the example of Jesus Christ. He writes: "For ye know the grace of our Lord Jesus Christ, that, though he was rich, yet for your sakes he became poor, that ye through his poverty might be rich."[18] We shall experience some difficulties if we attempt to be too specific about the details of this verse. But the general meaning of the verse is clear. The love of God in Christ has expressed itself in the great sacrifice. God has so loved that He has given His only begotten Son. The love of Christ has led Him to lay aside His heavenly glory, to enter our earthly life, and to die on the cross for the sins of the world. Through His great act of redemptive love Jesus has made us rich. He has opened the way for us to lay hold of the inheritance, incorruptible, and undefiled, and that fadeth not away, reserved in heaven for us.[19] The springs of Christian giving are always to be found in the great redemptive act in which God gives Himself.

8. *Equality Based on Love*

Paul is concerned that through the readiness of Christians to share with their brothers in need there may be created in the church a rough equality based on love. He writes, "I mean not that other

---

[17] II Corinthians 8:5.
[18] II Corinthians 8:9.
[19] I Peter 1:4.

men be eased, and ye burdened: but by an equality, that now at this time your abundance may be a supply for their want, that their abundance also may be a supply for your want: that there may be equality."[20] The equality which Paul envisions here is not the equality in which the goods of a community are pooled and divided equally among all the members of the community. His equality is rather that of a big family in which those who are more prosperous stand behind those who are needing help, and expect in turn to receive help should the positions be reversed. The Christian community is to Paul a great brotherhood. And the visible expression of the reality of that brotherhood is to be found in an equality based on love. The need of this kind of sharing within the Christian community is just as vital in the church today as it was when Paul penned his letter to the Corinthians.

9. Spiritual Compensations

In the closing part of the ninth chapter of II Corinthians, Paul points out the compensations of Christian stewardship. He reminds the Corinthians that the rewards they will reap will be in proportion to the way in which they have sowed. He says, "But this I say, He which soweth sparingly shall reap also sparingly; and he which soweth bountifully shall reap also bountifully."[21] In the next verse he describes the characteristics of the Christian giver as he says, "Every man according as he purposeth in his heart, so let him give; not grudgingly, or of necessity: for God loveth a cheerful giver." He returns immediately to his theme of the compensations that go with Christian stewardship as he says, "And God is able to make all grace abound toward you; that ye, always having all sufficiency in all things, may abound to every good work . . . being enriched in every thing to all bountifulness, which causeth through us thanksgiving to God."

God's Unspeakable Gift

Having stated the rewards that go with Christian giving, Paul lets his mind play on the larger purposes which he expects to accomplish in the church through the offering he is promoting. He says, "The administration of this service not only supplieth the want of the saints, but is abundant also by many thanksgivings unto God;

[20] II Corinthians 8:13, 14.
[21] II Corinthians 9:6.

while by the experiment of this ministration they glorify God for your professed subjection unto the gospel of Christ, and for your liberal distribution unto them, and unto all men; and by their prayer for you, which long after you for the exceeding grace of God in you. Thanks be unto God for his unspeakable gift."[22] The picture that Paul sets before us here is filled with beauty. He knows, of course, that the administration of his offering will supply the wants of the saints. He knows also the deep prejudice between Jew and Gentile. He has sought to build a church in which this prejudice is overcome. But he knows the deep suspicion with which many of the Jewish Christians at Jerusalem look upon the Gentiles who have entered the Christian church. In this situation, he sees the consequences of the offering which he expects to bear to Jerusalem. He has a vision of the saints at Jerusalem as they glorify God for the subjection of the Gentiles to the gospel of Christ. He hears the prayers which the Christians in Jerusalem will offer for their brothers among the Gentiles because of the grace of God which has fallen on the Gentile churches. And as this vision grips his soul, Paul himself lifts his heart to God and cries out, "Thanks be unto God for his unspeakable gift." In a careless examination of this passage we might think that the unspeakable gift which Paul mentions here is His gift of Jesus Christ. The gift of His only begotten Son is the greatest gift that God can ever give to man. But Paul in this passage is not thinking of God's gift of His Son. The thing that calls forth the rapture of Paul's soul here is the exceeding grace of God which has fallen upon the churches of Macedonia, Achaia, and Galatia. And the context tells us at once what this grace is. The unspeakable gift of God is the grace of giving which at this moment has appeared in the Gentile churches. This has been God's way of preserving the unity of His church. This has been God's way of preparing His Church for her world task. And in the presence of this gift of God Paul bows his head and gives thanks to God for His unspeakable gift.

[22] II Corinthians 9:12-15.

QUESTIONS ON CHAPTER V

1. Show that at various times in his life Paul was interested in the raising of offerings for the saints at Jerusalem.
2. What was the double purpose that Paul had in all of these offerings?
3. What implications can we draw from the fact that Paul directed the Christians to take the offering on the first day of the week?
4. Are the churches right in their effort to make the offering an integral part of the worship service?
5. What reasons can you give in favor of Christian giving on a *weekly* basis?
6. Show that the obligation to give is in proportion to the way in which God has prospered us.
7. How did Paul tell the Corinthians they were to avoid having to complete the offering after his arrival?
8. How did Paul avoid laying himself open to the criticism of misusing the offerings he collected?
9. Is it a sound principle that in the handling of church finances we should take thought for things honest in the sight of men?
10. How would the application of this principle affect the way in which the finances of your church are handled?
11. What does Paul mean when he says that all the money collected in the churches should be spent to the glory of God?
12. How would the application of this principle affect the handling of money in your local church? in the financial program of your denomination?
13. Show that Paul had a carefully organized plan for the promotion of this offering in the churches.
14. Is promotional work of this kind still necessary in the church?
15. Make a list of the motives to which Paul appealed in the raising of this offering.

16. How does the giving of a people reveal the genuineness of their love?

17. Is it right in our promotion of Christian giving to appeal to the competitive motive?

18. Is there a danger in basing our appeal too largely on this motive?

19. What does Paul mean when he speaks of the "grace of God bestowed on the churches of Macedonia"? (II Corinthians 8:1.)

20. What does he mean when he urges the Corinthians to "abound in this grace also"? (II Corinthians 8:7.)

21. Should Christian giving root in the surrender of our whole personality to God in Christ?

22. Can the surrender of ourselves to Christ be complete if it does not affect our attitude toward our possessions?

23. How does Paul set before the Corinthian Christians the example of the sacrifice of Christ?

24. What are the implications for Christian giving of Paul's understanding of the Christian community as a brotherhood based on love?

25. What is the "unspeakable gift" to which Paul refers in II Corinthians 9:15?

CHAPTER VI

Fellowship in the Furtherance of the Gospel

The Philippians Followed Paul with Their Gifts

ONE of the reasons which Paul had for writing the letter to the Philippians was to thank the Christians at Philippi for the offering they had sent to Rome by the hand of Epaphroditus. This offering was not the first that Paul had received from this church. In the beginning of his ministry in Europe, the church at Philippi had been the only church to follow Paul with her gifts. But even during his stay at Thessalonica this church had sent more than once to his need. While Paul was in Prison at Rome, the Philippians had thought often of the great apostle but they had lacked the opportunity of sending to him until at last they were able to send their gift by the hand of Epaphroditus.

Giving as Fellowship in Preaching the Gospel

As Paul writes to thank the Philippians for their gift he says, "I thank my God upon all my remembrance of you . . . for your fellowship in furtherance of the gospel from the first day until now; being confident of this very thing, that he who began a good work in you will perfect it until the day of Jesus Christ."[1] In commenting on this passage, we should notice the difference in the translation in the King James and the American Standard Versions. In the King James Version, Paul thanks God for the fellowship of the Philippians in the gospel. In the American Standard Version, he thanks God for the fellowship of the Philippians in the *furtherance* of the gospel. The translation in the American Standard Version is the correct translation, and this brings out much more clearly Paul's idea. Paul is not talking here about the fellowship which he and the Philippians have experienced as Christians. That he did experience such a fellowship with the Christians at Philippi is not to be doubted. But in this passage Paul is thanking the Philippians for

[1] Philippians 1:3-6. (American Standard Version.)

the fellowship which they have had with him in the *furtherance* of the gospel; that is, in his great purpose of spreading all over the inhabited world the good news of what God had done in Jesus Christ.

When Paul refers to their "fellowship in furtherance of the gospel" his immediate reference is to the offering that the Philippians have sent to him. This offering represents to Paul the fellowship which these Philippian Christians have with him in the spread of the gospel. This is a unique and dynamic way in which to conceive of the offerings that are taken in the churches. It will be our purpose in this study to develop this idea and to show the accuracy with which it describes this aspect of Christian giving.

The idea of "fellowship in furtherance of the gospel" is a much more positive idea than the similar expression used in II Corinthians 8:4 in which Paul describes the offering which he was taking at that time as "fellowship in the ministering to the saints."[2] The two ideas are not to be clearly separated. Through his ministry to the saints Paul was working out the larger purpose of binding together the Jewish and the Gentile sections of the church. And even today the ministry of the church to human need is one of the most effective ways that we have of breaking down prejudice and preparing the way for the proclamation of the gospel. The work of medical missions is, for example, a form of ministry to human suffering but the medical missionary has been most effective in opening up new fields for Christian missions. But a program of ministering to human need does not strike at the roots of sin and evil unless it is accompanied by the proclamation of the gospel. Paul's passion to make Christ known to the ends of the earth struck much more deeply at the roots of human need than his passion to minister to the wants of the saints.

He Who Began a Good Work

As Paul thinks about the fellowship which these Christians at Philippi have had with him in the furtherance of the gospel, he makes some comments concerning the giving of the Philippians which reveal his deep understanding of the spirit of their giving. Paul thanks them for their fellowship in the furtherance of the gospel from the first day until now and adds, "Being confident of this very thing, that *he* who began a good work in you will perfect

[2] II Corinthians 8:4. (American Standard Version.)

it until the day of Jesus Christ."[3] We are left to our own imagination to supply the noun for the pronoun *he,* but it is obvious that the *he* refers to God. Paul is confident that it is God who has begun this good work among the Philippian Christians. The good work refers, of course, to the practice of the Philippian Christians in following Paul with their gifts.[4] When Paul fled from Philippi to Thessalonica, the Christians at Philippi were moved to send gifts to him. Through these gifts Paul was enabled to carry on more efficiently his ministry in Thessalonica. He felt that the gifts had come to him in Thessalonica because the God who was sending him forth to preach was moving in the hearts of the people at Philippi. Later in his ministry Paul was in Corinth. Here also he did not feel it was wise in the beginning to receive offerings from the people. Just as his funds were exhausted, the brethren from Macedonia arrived and supplied the measure of his want.[5] Paul felt that the God who had begun a good work among the Philippian Christians while he was at Thessalonica was still carrying on His work in the hearts of these Christians. The years passed. Paul was in prison in Rome. He was without funds and was disciplining himself in the matter of doing without the things he needed. Again the messenger of the Philippians arrived. And again Paul realized God's power to move through His church to the support of His servant.

Until the Day of Christ Jesus

Because Paul felt that God was at work in His church, he was convinced that this work would go on until the day of Christ Jesus. Paul was not sure whether or not he would survive until Christ came back. He was sure that God would continue to be at work in His church until the present dispensation was finished and Jesus

---

[3] Philippians 1:6. (American Standard Version. Italics ours.)

[4] The constant use of this text as a proof text for the doctrine of the perseverance of the saints is a striking illustration of the way in which we use the language of Scripture, apart from its context, to prove our points. We state a great Christian truth when we say that God who has begun His work of grace in the human heart will finish the work which He has started. Justification leads in the end to glorification. This doctrine can be soundly based on passages such as Romans 8:29; Jude 24; Hebrews 7:25; John 10:28, 29. But at best it is referred to in a very indirect way in the text before us.

[5] II Corinthians 11:8, 9.

Christ returned to bring to its glorious issue the divine purpose in history.

God at Work in the Church's Giving

The point of view that Paul had needs to be caught again in the church. The God who calls men and sends them forth to the mission field is the God who moves in the hearts of His people and calls His church to the support of the work that represents His will in the world today. The support of the great enterprises of the church roots deeper than the ever varying interests of an unstable people. Ultimately this support roots in the fact that God is able to work "a good work" in His church today even as He did in Paul's day. The leaders of the church arise and do their work and go on. The men who support the church in one generation will pass from the scene. But behind it all there is the eternal God who is at work in the world. He will continue the good work He has begun until the day of Christ Jesus.

Paul knows that the generosity of the Philippians roots in the power of God at work in the hearts of the Christians there. But Paul knows also that God does not work in a vacuum. Behind the giving of these Christians there is the fact that they have caught from Paul his passion for the spread of the gospel. The Christians in Philippi would never have given as they did if they had not found in Paul a man who had a great and contagious purpose. Religion is not so much taught as it is caught. Paul was possessed by a purpose so great and so dynamic that the men who were around him were certain to catch it too. And when men had caught Paul's purpose they could not rest until they had found a way to enter into fellowship with him in his great purpose to spread the gospel to the ends of the earth.

Paul's Missionary Passion

1. To the Ends of the Earth

Paul was a man with a missionary passion. He was one of those restless pioneers who could not rest while there was unevangelized territory he had not entered. He writes the Romans, "From Jerusalem and round about unto Illyricum, I have fully preached the gospel of Christ. . . . not where Christ was named, lest I should build upon another man's foundation . . . I have been much hindered from coming to you. But now having no more place in these parts, and having a great desire these many years to come unto you; whensoever I take my journey into Spain, I will come to you."[6] From Jerusalem to Illyricum and on to Rome and to Spain—the purpose of Paul covered the whole of the inhabited world as he knew it.

2. To All Races

But Paul's passion for the propagation of the gospel was more than the passion of a man who must move on and on. He was known as the Apostle unto the Gentiles. The gospel of the uncircumcision was committed unto him.[7] He had such a sense of his obligation to give the gospel to the Gentile world that he could cry out, "I am debtor both to the Greeks, and to the Barbarians."[8] But in every city he began his preaching with the message to the Jews. He could cry out, "Brethren, my heart's desire and prayer to God for Israel is, that they might be saved."[9] He could even say: "I could wish that myself were accursed from Christ for my brethren, my kinsmen according to the flesh."[10]

3. Woe Is Me If I Preach Not

Paul knew that a necessity was laid on him to preach the gospel. He could say, "For though I preach the gospel, I have nothing to glory of: for necessity is laid upon me; yea, woe is unto me, if I preach not the gospel!"[11] He tells us that he was approved of God to be intrusted with the gospel.[12]

Paul's Convictions as a Missionary

A great passion has to be based on great convictions. Paul was concerned to give the gospel to all men because he knew that the gospel was the only hope of salvation for a lost world. He knew that all men had sinned and come short of the glory of God.[13] He knew that all the world was guilty before God.[14] He knew that the

---

[6] Romans 15:19-24.
[7] Galatians 2:7.
[8] Romans 1:14.
[9] Romans 10:1.
[10] Romans 9:3.
[11] I Corinthians 9:16.
[12] I Thessalonians 2:4.
[13] Romans 3:23.
[14] Romans 3:19.

end of the way of sin was death.[15] But Paul knew that he was the bearer of a gospel that would meet the needs of a lost world. He could say, "I am not ashamed of the gospel of Christ: for it is the power of God unto salvation to every one that believeth; to the Jew first, and also to the Greek."[16]

Paul himself had passed through the experience of conversion. He could say, "This is a faithful saying, and worthy of all acceptation, that Christ Jesus came into the world to save sinners; of whom I am chief. Howbeit for this cause I obtained mercy, that in me first Jesus Christ might shew forth all longsuffering, for a pattern to them which should hereafter believe on him to life everlasting."[17] In the second chapter of this same book, he refers to God, our Saviour, "Who will have all men to be saved, and to come unto the knowledge of the truth. For there is one God, and one mediator between God and men, the man Christ Jesus; who gave himself a ransom for all, to be testified in due time. Whereunto I am ordained a preacher, and an apostle."[18]

The verses we have just quoted are packed with the great convictions that undergirded the passion of Paul for the furtherance of the gospel. He spoke out of the personal experience of his life. He was convinced that the Christ who had saved him could also save others. In fact, he thought of himself as a pattern of what God could do with a man lost in sin. He saw God's gracious purpose of salvation as this purpose reached to all men. He believed in the *one* God, and because he knew there was only *one* God, he knew that this one God was the God of *all* men everywhere. But Paul was perfectly clear as to where this one God had revealed Himself. He knew that there was *one* mediator between God and men. This mediator was the man Christ Jesus. To Paul the Mediator was fully God and fully man. And to him Christ's work as mediator centered in His death when He "gave himself a ransom for all." Paul knew that he stood close to that moment of history in which the great redemptive purpose of God was revealed. He knew that he had been ordained a preacher to give to both Jew and Gentile the knowledge of God in Christ.

---

[15] Romans 6:23.
[16] Romans 1:16.
[17] I Timothy 1:15,16.
[18] I Timothy 2:3-7.

F. B. Meyer has placed on the lips of Paul a little poem that reveals in some measure that mighty passion to preach Christ which was at the heart of the great apostle to the Gentiles.

"Oft when the word is on me to deliver,
Lifts the illusion and the truth lies bare;
Desert or throng, the city or the river,
Melts on a lucid paradise of air.

"Only like souls I see the folk thereunder,
Bound who should conquer, slaves who should be kings
Hearing their one hope with an empty wonder,
Sadly contented in a show of things.

"Then with a rush the intolerable craving
Shivers through me like a trumpet call,
Oh, to save these, to perish for their saving,
Die for their life, be offered for them all."[19]

In Romans, Paul defines in clear-cut terms the message he preached. He says, "If thou shalt confess with thy mouth the Lord Jesus, and shalt believe in thine heart that God hath raised him from the dead, thou shalt be saved. For with the heart man believeth unto righteousness; and with the mouth confession is made unto salvation. For the scripture saith, Whosoever believeth on him shall not be ashamed. For there is no difference between the Jew and the Greek: for the same Lord over all is rich unto all that call upon him. For whosoever shall call upon the name of the Lord shall be saved."[20] This statement of Paul's message is followed with a verse which reveals his great yearning that every man upon our earth should hear the message of salvation. He says, "How then shall they call on him in whom they have not believed? and how shall they believe in him of whom they have not heard? and how shall they hear without a preacher? and how shall they preach, except they be sent?"[21]

---

[19] Quoted in *The Marks of a Man,* by Robert E. Speer. (Page 110.)
[20] Romans 10:9-13.
[21] Romans 10:14, 15.

Fellowship in Prayer
Personal Work and Giving

When a great man is possessed by a great purpose, that man becomes a center of dynamic power. Those who knew Paul were forced to yield themselves to his message or to rebel violently against him. Those who followed Paul caught his spirit and shared his purpose. They sought inevitably to have fellowship with him in the furtherance of the gospel. Men could have fellowship with Paul in the furtherance of the gospel as they also set out to win men for Christ. The Pauline churches were centers of a dynamic and crusading Christianity. It was impossible for men to catch Paul's spirit without becoming men who were possessed by the passion to win others to Christ. But the personal work that was done by Paul's followers did not exhaust their desire to have fellowship with him in the furtherance of the gospel. Paul and his converts stood together in a fellowship of prayer. Paul's letters are filled with tender passages in which he reveals the way he bore the burden of the care of the churches in prayer to God. He prayed for the churches. He prayed constantly for his friends as individuals. And Paul's converts prayed with and for him. Through prayer the struggling churches scattered over the Roman Empire were bound into a great fellowship in Christ.

But the desire of the Philippian Christians for fellowship with Paul in the furtherance of the gospel was not exhausted in their fellowship with him in prayer. In fact, the reality of this fellowship in prayer with Paul in his great purpose was closely related to the will to express the interest of the church in some deed which gave concrete expression to the yearning expressed in the prayers of the people. The most effective way for the majority of the Philippian Christians to express their fellowship with Paul in his missionary purpose was through their giving. Through their giving they could release Paul from spending long hours at tentmaking and enable him to give his whole time to the propagation of the gospel. Through their giving they could enable him to rent a house in Rome and make this house the center of his efforts to evangelize the city.

The Larger Work

Paul did not work alone. He usually kept around him a large staff of active workers. In fact, a study of the men around Paul would make one of the most fascinating studies of people in the New Testament. Timothy and Titus were among his most trusted henchmen. During the later years of his life Luke was constantly with him. And the complete list of those around Paul would include such names as Tychicus, Epaphroditus, Epaphras, Aquila and Priscilla, Onesimus, Archippus, Demas, John Mark, Silas, Phoebe, etc. Paul was constantly sending these followers on missions for him which carried them all over the Roman Empire. Through them he kept in touch with the churches he had founded. Through them he exercised oversight both in doctrine and in discipline. But the men around Paul could not have been entirely self-supporting. There had to be money to pay the expenses of these men as he sent them on difficult missions in the interest of the growth of the church. It was the gifts of the Christians in churches like the church at Philippi which made it possible for Paul to support his helpers and carry on through them the larger work of evangelism.

Fellowship in the Tasks of the Kingdom Today

The principle set forth in Paul's relation to the Philippians is one of the dynamic principles of Christian giving. Men will give when their giving represents their fellowship with some great Christian who has won their confidence and their love. Men will give to a cause that has become incarnate in a man. They will not give in the same way to a benevolent budget. If it is to be effectively presented in the church, the benevolent budget must be personalized and made to live before the church as the fellowship of the church in the great enterprises of the Kingdom.

It is possible for the budget of the church to be presented today in terms of fellowship in the furtherance of the gospel. The gifts that go to pastor's salary and current expenses can be the fellowship of a people in the furtherance of the gospel. If through their gifts a congregation make it possible for their pastor to be free from worldly cares and avocations and able to give his whole time to preaching, pastoral work, etc., they are entering into fellowship with their minister in the proclamation of the gospel. The planting of an adequate church building in a strategic area of a city may be fellowship in the furtherance of the gospel.

The benevolent budget of a church can be interpreted in the same terms. The gifts of a congregation to Foreign Missions may be the fellowship of the people of the church with the men who have been willing to dedicate their lives to the actual preaching of the gospel in the foreign field. And it is usually true that wherever a church has gone forward in a large way in the support of Foreign Missions, it is because the people of that church have caught from a few spiritual leaders the passion for the evangelization of the world which has become incarnate in their lives. Giving to Foreign Missions may become a holy thing when it becomes fellowship with those who have caught a passion like that which Paul had for the evangelization of a lost world.

Gifts to Home Missions may become fellowship with those who are witnessing for Christ in the needy places of the homeland. Gifts to the great educational tasks of the church may be seen in the same light. The colleges and seminaries of the church are an essential part of the program of the church if she is to gird herself for her world task. Most of our great gifts to these causes have come from laymen who experienced a certain sense of fellowship with educators who were bearing in Christ's name the burden of the educational task of the church.

It is possible to follow this line of thinking through the whole budget of the church. No cause has a rightful place in the budget of a church that is not related directly, or indirectly, to the supreme task of the church, the furtherance of the gospel. We must never let our budget become so involved in debates over percentages that we fail to see behind all of these debates to the fellowship of the people of a congregation in the great causes of the Kingdom. And in most cases a congregation will not experience this sense of fellowship until they come into contact with men who are dominated by a great purpose which is based on great convictions.

Spiritual Victory—in Poverty or in Wealth

We have given the major portion of this chapter to the development of the understanding of giving as fellowship in the furtherance of the gospel. But as in this chapter our study is based primarily on Philippians, we should consider in closing the comments concerning this offering with which Paul concludes his letter. As he thanks the Philippians for this offering he writes, "Not that I speak in respect of want: for I have learned, in whatsoever state I am, therein to be content. I know how to be abased, and I know also how to abound: in everything and in all things have I learned the secret both to be filled and to be hungry, both to abound and to be in want. I can do all things in him that strengtheneth me."[22] In these verses Paul is thinking primarily of his capacity to live with little or with much. It took self-discipline for Paul to live on the very little that at times represented all that he had to go on. It took just as much self-discipline of a different sort for him to handle in a way that was Christian the large offerings that sometimes came to him. From this point of view, it is probably easier for a poor man to live as a Christian than it is for a rich man to so live that in all of his spending he is pleasing to God. One of the most quoted verses in Scripture is Philippians 4:13 in which Paul says, "I can do all things in him that strengtheneth me." We are justified in giving these words a larger application than their immediate setting. But we should remember that in the context of Philippians they refer primarily to Paul's capacity to live as a Christian whether with little or with much. And the real meaning of this passage is that on the basis of Paul's experience it gives to every Christian the promise that he will receive from Christ the power—regardless of the circumstances in which he finds himself—to be Christian in the handling of the things he has. This is not a little promise. One of the most difficult of the tasks which we face as Christians is the necessity that is laid upon us to so handle material things that we shall always be Christian in our attitudes toward our possessions. In Christ we can find the strength to resist the temptations that come through poverty. In Christ we can find also the strength to resist the temptations that come to us through wealth.

In verse 17, Paul says, "Not that I seek for the gift; but I seek for the fruit that increaseth to your account."[23] He is more concerned in the spiritual development of his people than he is in the size of their gifts. This should be the attitude of every true spiritual leader. The growth of the Philippians in the grace of giving was of deeper concern to Paul than his knowledge of what he could do with the gift they had sent.

A Sacrifice Acceptable to God

In verse 18, he describes their gift as "an odor of a sweet smell, a sacrifice acceptable, well-pleasing to God."[24] Perhaps Epaphroditus

---

[22] Philippians 4:11-13. (American Standard Version.)
[23] American Standard Version.
[24] American Standard Version.

talked over with Paul the story of the way in which the offering was raised. We can imagine that Paul saw behind this offering to the individual sacrifices that made it possible. He may have known the actual gifts given by Lydia, or by the Philippian jailer, or by the half-crazy girl he had healed. He may have known what these gifts cost the givers. As he contemplates the offering in this way he bursts forth in the language of Old Testament sacrifice. He sees in this offering something that is pleasing to God. An offering for the furtherance of the gospel which is born of the love, the devotion, and the sacrifice of a people is a worthy offering to lay on God's altar and with such an offering God is well pleased.

As Paul looks upon this offering he says to the Philippians, "And my God shall supply every need of yours according to his riches in glory in Christ Jesus."[25] We usually quote this text as a great promise, and we usually fail to notice the condition that underlies it. This promise is spoken to a people who have presented an offering which is to God as "an odor of a sweet smell, a sacrifice acceptable, well-pleasing to God." The people at Philippi have honored God with their substance, and because of this Paul is able to make to them the promise that his God will supply every need of theirs according to His riches in glory in Christ Jesus.

---

[25] American Standard Version.

QUESTIONS ON CHAPTER VI

1. Describe the way in which the Philippians followed Paul with their gifts.
2. Show that Paul describes the giving of the Philippians as their fellowship with him in the spreading of the gospel.
3. What does Paul mean when he says, "He who began a good work in you will perfect it until the day of Jesus Christ"?
4. How can we apply this idea to Christian giving today?
5. Describe Paul's missionary passion.
6. Discuss the convictions upon which Paul's missionary passion was based.
7. Discuss the ways in which the Philippians could express their fellowship with Paul in his passion for the furtherance of the gospel.
8. Why did Paul need money for the carrying out of his missionary program?
9. How is it possible to interpret the causes of the church today in terms of fellowship in the furtherance of the gospel?
10. What does Paul mean when he says, "I can do all things in him that strengtheneth me"?
11. How does Paul interpret Christian giving as "a sacrifice acceptable . . . to God"? Can all Christian giving be interpreted in this way?
12. What promise does Paul make to the Philippian Christians in Philippians 4:19? What is the spiritual condition of claiming this promise?

CHAPTER VII

The Support of the Christian Worker

SUPPORT FROM THE PHILIPPIANS

THE basis for some form of support for the Christian worker is involved in the studies we have already made. It appears particularly, for example, in the idea of *fellowship in the furtherance of the gospel.* The Philippians expressed their fellowship with Paul in his passion to spread the gospel by the gift that they sent him. This gift was used to pay Paul's expenses or to pay the expenses of some of the men whom Paul used as his messengers to the churches. The gift of the Philippians represented their fellowship in the furtherance of the gospel because it was used to meet some of the expenses involved in the program of evangelism which Paul was directing in Rome and from Rome to all parts of the Roman Empire.

THE BIBLICAL BACKGROUND

But while the idea of the support of the Christian worker is involved in all that we have said in the preceding chapters, we need to give a chapter to a more detailed consideration of the problems involved in the support of the Christians who give all or even a major part of their time to Christian work. That which has been implicit in the preceding chapters needs to be explicit. The truths which have been implied in all of our thinking need to be stated with a clarity that no one can misunderstand. In particular, we need to view this problem against the Biblical background; i. e., to examine the Biblical basis for the support of the ministry.

THE MINISTER AND THE CHRISTIAN WORKER

The problem which we are discussing in this chapter comes to a focus in the question of the support of the minister. As the church is organized today, every church must seek a pastor to be the leader of the church. For many of our smaller churches, the support of the preacher is the main item in their current expense. And even in our larger churches the question of the proper support of the pastor of the church is always a question of importance. But in our discussion of this problem as a part of our study of the teachings of Paul concerning Christian stewardship, we should remember that the distinction between ordained and unordained men was not fixed in the early church with the same clarity that it has now as it is seen against the whole background of ecclesiastical tradition. Many of those whom Paul used as his messengers were probably not ordained. The fundamental problem with Paul was the question of the support of those who were so absorbed in their spiritual labors that they were not able to earn their own support in full. In this chapter, therefore, we should keep in mind not only the problems which the church must face in the support of her ordained ministry, but also the whole question of financial compensation for various types of services that are rendered to the church. This would bring within the scope of our chapter the question of the support of church secretaries, of directors of church music, of directors of religious education, of caretakers of church property, etc. But as our problem does center in the support of the ministry we will first examine this problem in the light of Paul's teachings and then consider the question of the church as an employer of labor.

Paul Refuses Support

When we examine Paul's practice in the receiving of support from the churches, we seem to run into a dilemma. On the one hand we find Paul steadily arguing for the necessity of an adequate support for the ministry. On the other hand, we find him constantly referring to his refusal to receive a support. In his speech to the Ephesian elders, he says, "I have coveted no man's silver, or gold, or apparel. Yea, ye yourselves know, that these hands have ministered unto my necessities, and to them that were with me."[1] He writes to the Corinthians, "I have a stewardship intrusted to me. . . . That, when I preach the gospel, I may make the gospel without charge, so as not to use to the full my right in the gospel."[2] He refers to his refusal to receive help from the Corinthians when in II Corinthians he says, "And when I was present with you and was in want, I was not a burden on any man; for the brethren, when they came from Macedonia, supplied the measure of my want; and

[1] Acts 20:33, 34.
[2] I Corinthians 9:17, 18. (American Standard Version.)

in everything I kept myself from being burdensome unto you, and so will I keep myself."[3] He insists that when he visits them the third time he will follow the same policy and will not depend upon them for support.[4] It is evident that not only did Paul not receive support from the Corinthians, but that when the occasion demanded he was accustomed to calling attention to his refusal to receive such support. After referring to the way in which he had not let himself become a burden to the church in Corinth, he says, "As the truth of Christ is in me, no man shall stop me of this boasting in the regions of Achaia."[5]

Because passages like these are found in Paul's writings, the churches that believe in an unpaid ministry have at times sought to find in Paul's thinking support for their position of refusing to pay men for the preaching of the gospel. For this reason, these passages need to be examined with care. We need to ask ourselves why it was that Paul at times refused to receive support from the churches he was founding. We should notice that Paul, while he refused to receive help from the Christians at Corinth during the time of his ministry there, had no objection to receiving help from the churches of Macedonia during his ministry in Achaia. In fact, it was only because he did receive such help that he was able to get along without any assistance from the churches in Corinth.[6] And as we have seen in our study of Philippians, Paul was not above gently soliciting such help. And while Paul did not personally receive help from the Christians of Corinth, he brought strong pressure to bear on the Christians at Corinth in order to lead them to give to the offering he was taking for the suffering saints at Jerusalem. Paul himself tells us why he did not receive from the Corinthian Christians offerings for his own expenses. He says, "But what I do, that I will do, that I may cut off occasion from them which desire occasion."[7] Paul had many enemies. And his enemies were constantly seeking to find something that they might use against him. If Paul during the founding of the church at Corinth had received offerings that went to his own support, he would have made it possible for his enemies to say that the preaching of the gospel was to Paul a way of gain. Paul did not wish to place himself in a position in which his

---

[3] II Corinthians 11:9. (American Standard Version.)
[4] II Corinthians 12:14. (American Standard Version.)
[5] II Corinthians 11:10.
[6] II Corinthians 11:9.
[7] II Corinthians 11:12.

motives for preaching could be called in question. He writes to the Corinthians, "I will not be burdensome to you: for I seek not yours, but you."[8] He elaborates this idea as he says, "I will very gladly spend and be spent for you; though the more abundantly I love you, the less I be loved. But be it so, I did not burden you: nevertheless, being crafty, I caught you with guile. Did I make a gain of you by any of them whom I sent unto you? I desired Titus and with him I sent a brother. Did Titus make a gain of you? walked we not in the same spirit? walked we not in the same steps?" Titus was the man whom Paul had sent to the church at Corinth to develop the Corinthians in the grace of giving.[9] But evidently Paul had instructed Titus that he was to follow Paul's example and not receive any gifts for his personal support from the church at Corinth while he was promoting there the offering for the saints at Jerusalem.

The considerations which determined Paul's course in Corinth are still of great importance in the church. It is of supreme importance that the fundamental concern of those who proclaim the gospel should be the souls of men and not the possessions of men. Very often in the opening of a new field, it is still inexpedient to place any large emphasis on the offerings that are to be received. In many cases men who are doing difficult pieces of mission work must be supported by funds that are not raised on the field. The man who ministers in some of our fields today must say to his people, "I robbed other churches, taking wages of them, to do you service."[10] And the church today should constantly examine herself to be sure that she has held on to Paul's insight in which the passion for men is put above the passion for their possessions. It has not always been true that the church was as deeply interested in the poor as in the rich. Of course, the church that wins men for Christ must in time bring to bear on the Christian conscience the whole idea of Christian stewardship. But the church must constantly examine herself to be sure that she has put first things first and that her interest in people runs deeper than her interest in their possessions.

A Self-Supporting Ministry

Paul's example in working at times for his own support raises also for us the question as to whether there is a place in the church for

[8] II Corinthians 12:14.
[9] II Corinthians 12:15-18.
[10] II Corinthians 11:8.

a ministry in which men earn through their own labors either all or part of their own support. It is unquestionably true that in the beginning of the Christian church, many of the men who did the work of the ministry were men who earned all or part of their living through their own labors. And today there are still some denominations that do not believe in a paid ministry. The preaching in these churches is done by men who farm or carry on some kind of business as a means of support. And in many of our more highly organized churches the ministers supplement their salaries by farming or teaching or writing.

Can the Minister Today Be Expected to Support Himself?

When Paul had no more satisfactory way of obtaining his support he usually turned to tentmaking as a means of making a living. And as far as the Biblical conception of the ministry is concerned, there can be no objection to the minister's following a similar procedure today. Very often weak churches which cannot support their own minister have been adequately served by unordained men who received their support entirely apart from their ministry to the church. The fundamental objection to a ministry which must earn all or part of its own support comes from the nature of the task of the ministry today. The work of the ministry demands a man's full time. The program of the modern church makes heavy demands on the ministry. The minister of a church of any size or importance must give himself to a ministry of preaching, of promotional work, and of pastoral work which demands all the strength that he has. From the point of view of the church, it is unwise to train men for the ministry through long years of preparation, to put them in positions of responsibility in which the future of the church depends on the way in which they give themselves to their task, and then to ask that they give a large proportion of their time and strength to the earning of a living through work that has no relation to the task they are called to do. Paul could make tents if he had to. But we can be thankful that he did not have to put the main energy of life into the making of tents. Most ministers could, if necessary, enter the economic order and earn in one way or another a living for themselves and for those dependent upon them. But the church must save her spiritual leaders for their spiritual tasks.

While Paul did at times, as a matter of expediency, lay aside his right to receive his support from those to whom he ministered, he never failed to assert that right, both for himself and for the ministry as a whole. He writes to the Corinthians, "When I preach the gospel, I may make the gospel without charge, so as *not to use to the full my right* in the gospel."[11] After developing his argument for the support of the ministry he tells the Corinthians, "If others partake of this right over you, do not we yet more? Nevertheless we did not use this right; but we bear all things that we may cause no hindrance to the gospel of Christ."[12] As Paul thought through the whole situation in Corinth he thought that it might be a hindrance to the spread of the gospel for him to insist in Corinth on taking offerings for his own support. But he made it very clear to the Corinthians that he possessed this right and his decision not to use it was merely a matter of what he considered to be the wise policy for the present. And as he thought back on his whole experience at Corinth he was not sure that it had been for the best interests of the church at Corinth for the church there to have been relieved of the obligation of supporting him during his ministry in their midst. He feels that the church at Corinth was inferior to the other churches because of their failure to attain self-support during his ministry with them. And he asks them to forgive him the wrong he has done them in not forcing them to support their own work. Paul has given us a suggestion here that needs in some cases to be followed out. There are times when as a matter of expediency it is unwise for the Christians in a community to be expected to support in full the work that is carried on in their midst. Foreign Mission work must in the beginning be supported by the gifts of the home church. And many of our weaker churches in our mission fields need to receive some help from the stronger churches. It is a wise strategy of church building to use the general funds of the church to help the Christians in a promising community to get a start, or to place adequate buildings at strategic locations. But very often churches have been injured by not being forced to support their own work. Home Mission funds have been wasted in the sustentation of churches that ought to have achieved self-support. Mission money has been used to make permanent the overchurching

[11] I Corinthians 9:18. (American Standard Version. Italics ours.)
[12] I Corinthians 9:12. (American Standard Version.)

of many of our communities. And on the Foreign Mission fields we have been slow to learn the value of bringing churches to full self-support as soon as possible.

Paul established churches all over the Roman Empire. Most of his churches were self-supporting from the very beginning. It was probably as a part of his effort to lead his churches to support their ministers that Paul developed the argument for the right of the man who preaches the gospel to live of the gospel. In his letter to the Romans, he justifies the offering taken among the Gentiles for the Jews at Jerusalem by saying, "It hath pleased them of Macedonia and Achaia to make a certain contribution for the poor saints which are at Jerusalem. It hath pleased them verily; and their debtors they are. For if the Gentiles have been made partakers of their spiritual things, their duty is also to minister unto them in carnal things."[13] Paul states here the principle that it is proper for the Gentiles to express to the Jewish Christians their appreciation of the spiritual ministry they have received through their gifts to the Jewish Christians. In I Corinthians, he applies this principle to the right of the minister to receive his support from those to whom he ministers. He says, "If we have sown unto you spiritual things, is it a great thing if we shall reap your carnal things?"[14] The language that Paul uses here has probably been overworked, but the idea that it expresses is sound. Those who give themselves to a spiritual ministry have a right to receive a ministry in carnal things.

Paul states the same idea in Galatians as he writes, "Let him that is taught in the word communicate unto him that teacheth in all good things."[15] Immediately following this verse we have the great verse, "Be not deceived; God is not mocked: for whatsoever a man soweth, that shall he also reap."[16] It is proper to apply this verse to the whole moral life of man. God has so ordered His universe that men reap what they sow. But we should remember that this great verse was originally spoken to support the idea that the man who is taught in the word should share in all good things with the man who teaches. When men give to the support of their spiritual leaders they are sowing not to the flesh but to the Spirit.

---

[13] Romans 15:26, 27.

[14] I Corinthians 9:11.

[15] Galatians 6:6.

[16] Galatians 6:7.

In his first letter to Timothy, Paul says, "Let the elders that rule well be counted worthy of double honour, especially they who labour in word and doctrine. For the scripture saith, Thou shalt not muzzle the ox that treadeth out the corn. And, the labourer is worthy of his reward."[17] In his argument for the support of the elder who labors in word and doctrine, Paul appeals here to an Old Testament law[18] and to a saying of Jesus.[19] Both of them emphasize the essential justice in the laborer's receiving the reward of his labor in the things that are necessary for the support of his life.

Paul drops into his Old Testament background again when he argues the right of the Christian minister to receive a support from the example of a similar support received in the Old Testament dispensation. He says, "Do ye not know that they which minister about holy things live of the things of the temple? and that they which wait at the altar are partakers with the altar?"[20] In the Old Testament dispensation those who gave themselves to a ministry in connection with the Temple received their living from the gifts brought to the Temple.

It is in this connection that Paul writes, "Even so hath the Lord ordained that they which preach the gospel should live of the gospel."[21] This statement may be merely Paul's summary of what he understands to be the will of God. But when Paul says "the Lord," he is usually referring to Jesus Christ. And it is not impossible that Paul is preserving for us here a command of our Lord which was not preserved in this form in the Gospels. It is possible that Peter or John told Paul that during the days of His flesh Jesus Christ for the guidance of His church had laid down the great principle that "they which preach the gospel should live of the gospel."[22] But regardless of whether or not Paul preserves here a saying of Jesus, we can be confident that Paul expresses here the will of his Lord. The

---

[17] I Timothy 5:17.

[18] Deuteronomy 25:4.

[19] Luke 10:7.

[20] I Corinthians 9:13.

[21] I Corinthians 9:14.

[22] If this is a word of the Lord which is preserved in the writings of Paul, it takes its place along with that other saying of Jesus which is preserved for us in Paul's speech to the Ephesian elders when Paul quotes Jesus as saying, "It is more blessed to give than to receive." (Acts 20:35.) And we might add the comment that in this case the two sayings of Jesus which are preserved to us by Paul both deal with Christian stewardship.

Lord has ordained that they which preach the gospel should live of the gospel.

State Support and Support by Voluntary Giving

When we acknowledge the Scriptural basis of the argument for the support of the ministry we have not solved the question as to how this support is to be raised. In the history of the church as a whole there have been two basic answers to this question. In America, we are committed to the support of the church by voluntary gifts of the people. This is the only system that could function in America where there is no established church and where the principle of separation of church and state is generally accepted. But we in the Protestant Churches of America ought to be aware of the fact that many of the Protestant Churches in Europe have been established churches in which the support of the church came in part, at least, from taxes collected by the state. And we should remember that where the Roman Catholic Church has the power to do so she usually sets up an arrangement with the state whereby tax-collected money is contributed to the support of the church. This issue is not entirely settled in America, as the Roman Catholic Church in America is constantly agitating for the use of state money for the support of schools controlled by the church. And the Protestant Churches are experiencing great difficulty in giving to their own institutions an adequate support which will enable them to compete with the state-supported schools.

We cannot settle the whole question of the sources of the support of the church simply by a reference to the procedure of the churches that Paul founded. In the Jewish state, church and state were so interwoven that it was impossible to separate clearly the sources of their support. But the church of the New Testament was a persecuted church, a church which by the end of Paul's ministry was coming into open conflict with the Roman state. It is obvious that such a church had to be supported purely on the basis of the voluntary gifts of its members.

There are two fundamental objections to the state support of the church. The first is that the springs of Christian giving are usually dried up when the state steps in and begins to support the church with tax-collected money. The churches that have enjoyed state support have usually done very little to develop their people in the grace of giving. But the more fundamental objection to state support is that support in the end always involves control. The free churches have always been able to assume a much more independent attitude toward the state than the state-supported churches.

Local Support and Denominational Support

When we have accepted the principle that the church must depend for her support on the voluntary gifts of her people, we have not fully solved the question of the source of the support of the church. There remains the question as to whether the minister shall receive his support directly from the church he serves or whether the money collected from the churches shall be sent to some central source and then distributed with the needs of the whole church in mind. In most of the Protestant Churches, we follow a course which moves between the two extremes mentioned here. The local church is expected, wherever possible, to be entirely self-supporting. At the same time we do seek through our mission boards to create a common fund through which the strength of the whole church can be brought to bear on the places of greatest need and opportunity. The principle of the direct responsibility of each local church for the support of its work has in it many defects. But in spite of its defects it is probably a much sounder principle than any attempt to create a general fund from which the ministry as a whole would receive their support.

The Basis of the Minister's Salary

What should be the basis of the minister's salary? This is a most difficult question, and all that we can do is to suggest some of the lines along which it has been approached. Probably the soundest principle in determining what the salary of the minister ought to be is that which is expressed in the terms of the call when the congregation agree to pay the minister a salary that will enable him to be free from worldly cares and avocations. And it is not possible to say in advance just what salary is necessary to meet this goal. The cost of living varies in different places and in different periods. The expenses which ministers have to meet vary with the size of their families and with the obligations made on them by the churches they are serving.

In actual practice, a good many factors enter into the determining of the size of the minister's salary. An obvious factor is the ability of the congregation to raise the salary. Many salaries are too small to meet the goal of leaving the minister free from worldly cares and avocations and free to give himself to his spiritual task. But very often the salaries represent the best that the church can do in the light of the obligations the church has to meet. On the other hand, there are some rich churches which pay salaries that seem to go beyond the standard of a support sufficient to leave the minister free to do his work. Before passing judgment concerning these salaries, we should remember that churches which pay the larger salaries are usually churches in which the financial demands on the minister are very heavy. It is important that all of our ministry should be sufficiently free from worldly cares and avocations to be able to give themselves to their spiritual task. But it is particularly imperative that those who carry the load of our great churches should be free to give themselves without reserve to the task that is laid upon them.

In the business world, the salary is determined largely on the basis of worth. A man is supposed to be paid on the basis of his value to the company he serves. But we must apply this principle with caution in our effort to determine the salary of the minister. In the ministry as in other walks of life, the inefficient man is often the most expensive man. A church will usually find it easier to pay an able man an adequate salary than to pay an incompetent man a much smaller salary. But this principle is not a sound principle for the determining of the salary of the minister. The salary of the minister should be thought of in terms of subsidy rather than compensation. The church is in business for service, not profit. And the tendency of the churches to evalute ministers in terms of the financial worth of their services is dishonoring to the ministry as a whole.

The Minister and the Sin of Covetousness

The churches need to pitch their whole attitude toward the salary of the minister on a more definitely spiritual plane. And the ministers of our churches need to be constantly on their guard lest they themselves fall into the sin of covetousness. The man who has answered the call of God to give himself to the proclamation of the gospel of Christ should be a man in whom the love of Christ has conquered the love of gain. Other men in other professions may think of their professions primarily as a means of making a living.[32] But the minister

[28] We take a very low view of the professions when we interpret them in terms of the money that can be made through them. No good doctor or teacher or lawyer would interpret his work in this way.

is called of God to the preaching of the gospel. In his choice of his work he has a right to consider the salary basis only as the size of the salary does bear on the way in which he can be free from worldly cares and avocations and able to give his full strength to his God-given work.

In his personal handling of his finances, the minister should strive to so live that he sets an example to all the people of God. He should spend on himself and on his family when such spending is necessary, if he is to be free to give himself to his task; but he should spend on himself and his family only as he is convinced that he can best serve the larger interests of the Kingdom of God by spending his money in this way. He should live simply in order that he may be able to give liberally. He should be ready at all times to give an account to God of his stewardship of the money that has come to him. In the sixth chapter of I Timothy, Paul makes a profound study of the spiritual dangers involved in false attitudes toward wealth.[24] At the end of this passage Paul turns to Timothy and says, "*But thou, O man of God,* flee these things."[25] This advice of Paul's might well become the motto of every minister as he faces the spiritual perils involved in false attitudes toward wealth.

The Church as Employer of Labor

In this chapter we have thought in terms of the support of the minister, but the principles we have discovered in the teachings of Paul with regard to the support of the minister should apply with equal force to the support of other Christian workers. We must be careful not to commercialize the work of the church. In every church in which the people have a mind to work, a vast amount of work will be done by the people of the church without any thought of financial compensation. The teaching of our Sunday schools is done largely on a volunteer basis. Much of our church music is on the same basis. In fact, one function of the church in a community is that the church gives to the people of the community an opportunity for service which they would not otherwise have. In many churches, apart from the salary of the minister, the whole work of the church is carried on on a volunteer basis.

While this is true in the smaller churches, many of the larger churches do find it necessary to employ additional persons for the

---

[24] Chapters VIII and IX of this book are based on this passage.
[25] I Timothy 6:11.

promotion of the work of the church. The work of these churches is so complex that they must have church secretaries, directors of religious education, directors of music, caretakers for the church plant, etc. And if the church calls men or women to give all or the major part of their time to the service of the church she should feel the same obligation for their support that is felt for the salary of the minister.

The church is an employer of labor. Many of those whom she employs are called to definitely Christian tasks. Many others are employed in tasks that are not essentially different from the ordinary tasks of labor. In the service of the church, men work as stenographers, as clerks, as sextons, as carpenters, as architects. Through her church-related schools and colleges the church employs teachers and educators. And the church as an employer of labor should see to it that her treatment of her labor is controlled by Christian standards. In her treatment of those who work for her, the church should set an example to all other employers of labor.

QUESTIONS ON CHAPTER VII

1. What reasons does Paul give for his refusal at times to receive support from the churches?

2. Discuss the conditions under which Paul was willing to receive support from the churches.

3. Show that Paul did receive such support from the Philippian church.

4. Do situations arise today in which it is either impossible or unwise for the Christian worker to receive his support from those to whom he ministers?

5. Why do some denominations believe in an unpaid ministry?

6. What objection would there be to the idea of an unpaid ministry for all of our churches?

7. Why did Paul feel that he had wronged the Corinthian church in not permitting this church to support him while he was working in Corinth?

8. How does Paul develop his argument to show that those who preach the gospel have the right to live of the gospel?

9. What are the objections to the idea of the support of the church through state-collected taxes?

10. How was the money for the support of the minister raised in the Pauline churches?

11. What advantages, if any, can you see in the idea of the support of the church by state-collected taxes?

12. Why was it that the churches of Europe held on for so long to state support?

13. What is the attitude of the Roman Catholic Church toward state support?

14. What should be the basis for the determining of the size of a minister's salary?

15. Would the principles that have been worked out as the basis for the support of the ministry apply to any other full-time Christian worker?

16. Discuss the church as an employer of labor.

CHAPTER VIII

The Love of Money As a Root of All Evil

Spiritual Dangers in False Attitudes Toward Wealth

PAUL writes to Timothy, "The love of money is the root of all evil: which while some coveted after, they have erred from the faith, and pierced themselves through with many sorrows."[1] In the preceding chapters we have interpreted giving in terms of "fellowship in the ministering to the saints" or in terms of "fellowship in furtherance of the gospel." But entirely apart from any concern for the support of her ministry in the world, the church must deal with the attitudes which men take to money, because false attitudes toward the getting and spending of wealth lie at the root of many of the greatest evils that afflict mankind. Paul understood the way in which those who desired to be rich could "fall into temptation and a snare, and into many foolish and hurtful lusts, which drown men in destruction and perdition."[2] In the first letter to Timothy, and in various other passages scattered through his Epistles, Paul warns Christians against the dangers to their spiritual life involved in false attitudes toward money. It is our purpose in this chapter to outline this treatment and to show the way in which Paul's warnings apply with equal force to Christians in the modern world.

The LOVE of Money Is a Root of All Kinds of Evil

The sentence, "The love of money is the root of all evil," is quoted from the King James Version. Of course, the statement in this form is obviously not true. The love of money is not the root of all evil. The evil that is present in human life roots much deeper than the love of money. Evil roots in the pride of man, in the rebellion of man against God, in the refusal of man to find the center of his life in God. The false attitudes which men assume toward money

[1] I Timothy 6:10.
[2] I Timothy 6:9.

are expressions of the more fundamental sins of pride and rebellion against God. The love of money is not the root of all evil and Paul never said that it was. To be understood, this text needs to be studied in the translation of it which is given in the American Standard Version. This translation reads, "The love of money is a root of all kinds of evil." We need to distinguish between *money* and the *love of money*. Money is not the root of all evil. It is the *love* of money which is one of the roots of evil. Paul wanted money because he knew that through the proper use of money he could release stored-up human energy to the building of the Kingdom of God. And in the letters to Timothy, Paul gives a number of positive suggestions as to the way in which money may be dedicated to the service of God. It is our purpose to balance this chapter with a much more positive chapter in which we study the way in which a Christian can use his money for purposes that are in harmony with the will of God. In this way the most consecrated servant of God may be keenly alive to the need of dedicated wealth as the basis for the support of the work of the church in the world. No Christian should be oblivious to the things that can be done through the dedication of wealth to high and noble purposes. But it is true that a false love of money may become a root of every kind of evil.

The Love of Money Is A Root of All Kinds of Evil

There is a vast difference between saying that the love of money is *the* root of all evil and saying that the love of money is *a* root of all evils. The great social evils do not root in the love of money alone. They root in many of the lusts of men. Commercialized prostitution roots in part in the love of money. It roots also in the whole perversion of the sex life in which men and women refuse to express their sex life within the limits laid down in the Word of God. Graft in politics roots in part in the love of money. It roots also in the lust for power. The evils which are connected with the liquor industry root in part in the love of money. They root even more deeply in the uncontrolled thirsts of men. No one can maintain that the love of money is *the* root of all evil. We can maintain that the love of money is *one* of the roots of all kinds of evil.

The Love of Money Is a Root of ALL KINDS of Evil

This brings us to a consideration of the closing word in the sentence we are examining. The Greek uses the plural word, *evils*.

We are not thinking here so much of evil as a unity as of the various forms in which evil appears in our world. The word is used in the distributive rather than in the collective sense. And the translators have sought to catch this thought by translating it "all kinds of evil." The problem of evil goes much deeper than the matter of a false attitude toward money. But when we go behind the various forms in which evil manifests itself in our world, we shall find that the love of money is one of the roots of almost every kind of evil.

The Hope of Their Gains Was Gone

In his personal experience, Paul had abundant opportunity for observing the way in which the love of money could become the root of every kind of evil. When he was at Philippi, Paul was used of God to bring healing and sanity to a "certain damsel possessed with a spirit of divination . . . which brought her masters much gain by soothsaying."[3] And Luke tells us that "when her masters saw that the hope of their gains was gone, they caught Paul and Silas, and drew them into the marketplace unto the rulers, and brought them to the magistrates, saying, These men, being Jews, do exceedingly trouble our city, and teach customs, which are not lawful for us to receive, neither to observe, being Romans."[4] Paul was permitted to preach undisturbed in Philippi until Christianity began to strike at the gain which evil men made from the infirmity of a poor girl. But when the owners of the girl possessed with the spirit of divination saw that the hope of their gains was gone, they began at once to arouse the mob against Paul. In their cries to the mob, they conceal their real motive. They appeal to race prejudice as they cry out that these men being Jews are teaching customs which it is not lawful for Romans to observe. But behind the hue and cry of the mob there are a few evil men who realize that the hope of their gains is gone.

Sirs, by This Craft We Have Our Wealth

A similar experience awaited Paul at Ephesus. Through the preaching of Paul, Christianity spread in Ephesus until it became a mass movement in all that section of Asia. An indirect tribute to the extent of the spread of Christianity is to be found in the decrease in the sale of the silver images of the goddess Diana, of the Ephe-

---

[3] Acts 16:16.
[4] Acts 16:19-21.

sians. The selling of these silver images was a profitable business to the silversmiths of Ephesus. As the sale of the images continued to fall off, Demetrius, a silversmith, gathered together the craftsmen and said to them, "Sirs, ye know that by this craft we have our wealth." There follows a speech in which Paul is condemned for saying "that they be no gods, which are made with hands." Demetrius goes on to say, "Not only this our craft is in danger to be set at nought; but also that the temple of the great goddess Diana should be despised, and her magnificence should be destroyed, whom all Asia and the world worshippeth."[5] Soon the town is filled with a mob which shouts, "Great is Diana of the Ephesians." The appeal to the mob is based on religious prejudice. But behind the cries of the mob there is a group of men who are arousing the mob because the craft through which they have their wealth is threatened. These men have their wealth through a craft which exploits the inveterate tendency of men to worship idols. But whenever Christianity has touched the craft through which evil men have their wealth it has been certain to arouse violent opposition. And this opposition usually conceals its real motive and hides behind appeals to race feeling or religious prejudice.

The Hope of a Bribe

Paul saw the corrupting power of the love of money among the officials of the Roman Empire. When Paul was arrested in Jerusalem, he was tried before Felix, the Roman governor of Caesarea. Felix soon became convinced of Paul's innocence of any charges that were worthy of prison or death. But he did not set Paul at liberty. In this action he was controlled in part by the willingness to show the Jews a favor. But one of his reasons for keeping Paul bound was the hope that "money should have been given him of Paul, that he might loose him."[6] Felix was willing to leave a man whom he knew to be innocent in prison in the hope that in the end he would receive a bribe to release him.

The Slave Trade

When Paul said that the love of money could become the root of every kind of evil, he spoke out of his own experience. And when we analyze the life of the modern world, we are amazed at the

---

[5] Acts 19:27.
[6] Acts 24:26.

extent to which the love of money continues to be one of the roots of almost every kind of evil. The love of money is one of the roots of practically every great social evil. The slave trade violated all of the fundamental rights of mankind. In this trade, helpless men and women were herded into ships like cattle and sold on the market to the highest bidders. But the difficulty in the abolishing of the slave trade lay in the fact that this trade was immensely profitable. One of the roots of the tragic War Between the States in America was slavery. Slavery was abolished without difficulty in the North because in the North it was not profitable. And slavery was on its way out in the South until the invention of the cotton gin made slavery profitable in the South.

Race Hatred

Race hatred remains one of the constant sources of trouble in America. Race prejudice does not root in economics alone. But unquestionably one of the roots of race prejudice is the fear of economic competition. This is true of the attitude of the white race toward the Chinese and Japanese on the west coast and the Negro in the South.

Slum Housing

In most of our large cities, inadequate housing is one of the major roots of crime. When children are raised in congested slum areas, they have little chance for a normal development. But the housing conditions that are found in the slums of our cities root in economic causes. They root in the fact that in normal times a large proportion of the people receive wages which are so low that they cannot afford to rent the more desirable houses. They root also in the acknowledged fact that the rate of return on money invested is particularly good when money is invested in cheap houses. If we dig down to the sources of the wealth of the upper classes we shall find that some of those who live in fine homes in the best residential sections are deriving a part of their living from the rent of houses that are the breeding place of crime. And all too often it is the money of the rich which is used to support the lobbies that prevent an effective effort on the part of city governments to clean up their slum areas. Here again the love of money is one of the roots of a great social evil.

Gambling

We have already mentioned the way in which the love of money lies as one of the roots of commercialized prostitution, of the various corruptions inevitably associated with the liquor industry, and of graft in politics. To these recognized evils, there should be added the various forms of gambling which permeate the country. The gambling evil roots in the love of money, in the desire to get something for nothing. It is one of the temptations into which men fall when they are minded to be rich without any great concern as to the sources of their wealth.

War

Modern war is an evil which threatens the very existence of civilization. We would simplify our problem entirely too much if we would say that modern wars are fought entirely over economic issues. Wars root in race feeling, in religious prejudice, in national ambitions, in the lust for power of men and groups, etc. And the use of force by governments to maintain order and to protect the basic rights of mankind is not necessarily an evil. But no student of history can be blind to the extent to which wars do root in economic causes. Wars are fought because of the economic rivalry of nations. They are fought to gain access to markets and to raw materials. They are fought to keep open the avenues of trade. They are fought because the strong nations wish permanently to exploit the weaker nations. It is fair to say that a false attitude toward money is one of the major roots of modern war.

Advertising of Alcoholic Beverages

A similar case can be made out in many other areas of our life. An obvious case in point is the advertising of alcoholic drinks which goes on in the press and over the radio. The makers of alcoholic beverages are willing to spend vast sums in this advertising because they know that they will get this money back in increased sales. The whole purpose of such advertising is to increase the consumption of alcoholic beverages. Everyone knows that this is an antisocial aim. Without raising again the discussion as to the legalizing of the sale of alcoholic beverages, it is obvious that a government that is interested in the welfare of its people should also be interested in keeping the consumption of alcoholic beverages to a minimum. And of course the advertising of such beverages can be controlled. In the very nature of the case, advertising is public and open to control. But when a large percentage of the advertising income of the press and the radio comes from the advertisements of alcoholic beverages, it becomes increasingly difficult to get effective government action against this evil. Here again the love of money is a major root of a great social evil.

Commercialization of the Sabbath

A similar case can be made out against the commercialization of the Sabbath. The observance of Sunday as a holy day set aside for rest and worship is one of the foundations of American life. It is one of the bulwarks of true religion. And unquestionably it is the love of money which is one of the roots of the increasing commercialization of the Sabbath that is going on in the life of America. Here again the real issue is concealed behind a front in which many humanitarian motives are advanced. But if, for example, the owners of the moving picture shows would find that over a period of time they were operating at a loss on Sunday, we would soon find that the moving picture industry would lose interest in the promotion of Sunday movies.

Corruption of Entertainment

The love of money lies also at the root of the immorality that is displayed to the American public through the moving picture industry. The only justification for shows which feature sex, and crime, and drinking is that the producers of these films feel that such pictures will be profitable. If the directors of this industry could be convinced that clean pictures were more profitable than immoral pictures, the reform of the moving picture industry could be accomplished.

Godliness as a Way of Gain

When we dig into the social evils of America, it is painful to realize the way in which false attitudes toward money have corrupted the whole fabric of our national life. Our social fabric is rotten at many points because we have put the demand for wealth above our interest in moral issues and in human rights. Unfortunately, we do not recognize the way in which the same love of money has a tendency to corrupt the finer things in our national life. In the chapter we are studying, Paul reminds us that there are many men who suppose that *godliness is a way of gain.* When Peter and John went to Samaria they found there a man named Simon who was a sorcerer. This man observed the tremendous effect of the coming of the Holy Spirit on the Christians at Samaria. He was probably the first man to see the possibility of turning Christianity into a way of gain. But he was not the last man to interpret godliness primarily as a way of gain. The line between a true and a false attitude here is very close. As Paul says, godliness with contentment is great gain. And as we saw in our last chapter, Paul argues for the right of those who preach the gospel to live of the gospel. But two illustrations will bring out the way in which the love of money can corrupt holy things. The first of these moves in the field of evangelism. The evangelist is called to a holy task. It is his duty to call men to surrender to the word of God in Christ. And it is entirely proper that the man who gives his entire time to evangelism should receive from those to whom he ministers a support which leaves him free to give his attention to his work. But some men have discovered that evangelism can be very profitable. And evangelism is beset with the constant danger that some evangelists will become more concerned with the offering they receive than with their spiritual ministry. The promotion of evangelism has at times been turned into a religious racket. The use of the radio for religious purposes has been corrupted in the same way. Religion will always remain one of the major interests of mankind. Unfortunately there are some men who have learned to prey upon this interest and to grow rich through the use of the radio for religious purposes. Here again the love of money has degraded the character of the programs that are presented in the name of religion to the American public over the radio.

The Pride of Wealth

It is comparatively easy to trace the way in which false attitudes toward wealth become the roots of social evils. It is not always as easy to see the way in which the possession of wealth has a tendency to undermine the spiritual life. In his letter to Timothy, Paul points out some of the dangers that are apt to be associated with the possession of riches. He tells Timothy to charge "them that are rich in this world, that they be not *highminded*."[7] A constant danger involved in the possession of wealth is that it will lead to pride and arrogance. The man who has material riches has much to set him apart from the masses of the people. He can live in the best type of home in the most desirable residential section. He can drive a big car. He can

---

[7] I Timothy 6:17.

command social advantages for himself and his children. He can command the services of others. He can dress in a way that sets him apart from other men. The danger involved in all this is that the possession of wealth will lead to "highmindedness," to pride, to arrogance. All honor to those Christians who have combined the possession of wealth with the preservation of simplicity in living and humility of spirit. But every man who has observed constantly the social attitudes of the rich knows that Paul has not overstated the case when he associates the temptation to "highmindedness" with the possession of wealth. And at times the social attitudes among the children of the rich are as deeply perverted as the social attitudes of the children of the slums who are embittered because of the poverty in their surroundings.

The Trust in Riches

Paul carries this thought a step further when he urges Timothy to charge the rich not to have their hope set on the uncertainty of riches but on God who giveth us richly all things to enjoy.[8] The spiritual danger involved in the possession of riches is that the basic trust of life will be placed in things rather than in God. This was the danger that Jesus saw in the life of the rich young ruler. For this reason Jesus placed His finger on the thing that stood between this man and the surrender of his life to God which constituted living faith. And when the young man turned away sorrowful because he had great possessions, Jesus said to His disciples, "Children, how hard is it for them that trust in riches to enter into the kingdom of God!"[9] There is so much that wealth does for us. If we have enough money, we can have food and clothing, and lands, and houses, and medical attention, etc. It is possible to go behind these things to a basic trust in the God who giveth us all things richly to enjoy. Those who have riches are always aware of moral values that money cannot buy. All men know at times the narrow limits within which the possession of wealth can minister to the needs of man. But the possession of wealth is apt to obscure these things. The man who has much goods laid up for many years is the man who is able to say to himself, "Take thine ease, eat, drink, and be merry."[10] Perhaps the greatest spiritual danger connected with the possession

---

[8] I Timothy 6:17.
[9] Mark 10:24.
[10] Luke 12:19.

of riches is that almost unconsciously men will come to depend on them in such a way that a life of complete dependence upon God is no longer possible.

Covetousness as Idolatry

Paul states this truth in a more positive fashion when he declares that covetousness is idolatry.[11] He tells the Corinthians not to keep company with any man who is named a brother who is a fornicator, or covetous, or an idolater.[12] He writes to the Ephesians, "For this ye know, that no . . . covetous man, who is an idolater, hath any inheritance in the kingdom of Christ and of God."[13] At first thought we do not always realize the way in which covetousness becomes an idolatry. The man who is dominated by the love of money does not consciously reject the God of the Bible for the worship of money. The covetous man can usually remain in good and regular standing in the church. But in the long run the thing that rules our life is the thing we worship regardless of the professions we may make to the contrary. If the dominating desire of a man's life is fixed on the accumulating of material possessions, it follows inevitably that in that man's life covetousness has become an idolatry. From this point of view we can see that covetousness may become one of the most dangerous idolatries in the life of the modern world. The Greeks used to personify the great human interests. Zeus was the god of power. Minerva was the goddess of wisdom. Venus was the goddess of love. In the same way, the word Mammon has come to stand for the god of wealth. We are not so naïve today as to suppose that there are gods who actually correspond to these names. But the dominating desire of our life remains our god. It is possible for the desire for wealth to so master us that this passion becomes the denial of the lordship of Jesus Christ in our life. From this point of view Jesus saw the inevitable contradiction between trust in riches and trust in God. He told His followers that they could not have a divided loyalty. He said to them, "No man can serve two masters . . . Ye cannot serve God and mammon."[14] Probably the most deadly idolatry in American life is the tendency of men to become so dominated by the desire for wealth that they cannot yield themselves in love and obedience to God in Christ.

---

[11] Colossians 3:5.
[12] I Corinthians 5:11.
[13] Ephesians 5:5.
[14] Matthew 6:24.

The Covetous Cannot Inherit the Kingdom of God

Paul says that the covetous man who is an idolater cannot have any inheritance in the Kingdom of Christ and of God.[15] His first reference here is probably to the experiences which men may have of God in Christ within our earthly life. When men are consumed by covetousness they have closed the door to the richer spiritual experiences which the Christian within this world may have in Christ. But the words of Paul must inevitably have a reach that goes beyond our earthly life. Man is mortal. But man is more than mortal. Every man has an immortal soul. Paul knows that it is possible for a man to so live within his earthly pilgrimage that when he comes to the end of this present life there is laid up for him a crown of righteousness.[16] He shares with Peter the Christian's hope of "an inheritance incorruptible, and undefiled, and that fadeth not away, reserved in heaven."[17] And to Paul the supreme tragedy of our earthly life would be for a man to be so absorbed with the material goods of a perishing world that he failed to lay hold of the eternal inheritance which God had prepared in Jesus Christ. And Paul makes it perfectly clear that the man who is mastered by covetousness has no inheritance in the Kingdom of God.

O Man of God, Flee These Things

If the church of Jesus Christ is to deal faithfully with men, she must deal fearlessly with the attitudes they take toward their material possessions, because a wrong attitude toward the getting and spending of wealth may become a root of every kind of evil. And covetousness if persisted in may at last shut a man out of the Kingdom of God. Perhaps this is what Paul meant when he said, "They that will be rich fall into temptation and a snare, and into many foolish and hurtful lusts, which drown men in destruction and perdition."[18] Perhaps he spoke from the personal observation of his life when he described those who had coveted after money until "they . . . erred from the faith, and pierced themselves through with many sorrows."[19] And against this background we can understand his injunction to Timothy as a word of warning to every Christian, "But thou, O man of God, flee these things."[20]

---

[15] Ephesians 5:5.
[16] II Timothy 4:8.
[17] I Peter 1:4.
[18] I Timothy 6:9.
[19] I Timothy 6:10.
[20] I Timothy 6:11.

QUESTIONS ON CHAPTER VIII

1. Show that entirely apart from the necessity of raising money to minister to human need and to further the spread of the gospel, the church deals with the attitudes of men toward wealth as a part of her whole spiritual ministry.
2. Criticize the statement of Paul in I Timothy 6:10—"The love of money is the root of all evil." How does the translation in the American Standard Version bring out the meaning of this text more accurately?
3. Show that Paul in his own experience was familar with the way in which the love of money could become a root of every kind of social evil.
4. List the illustrations given in this chapter in which the love of money is recognized as a root of social evils. Do you agree with this list? If not, what would you leave out? In addition to the things mentioned here, can you give other ways in which the love of money becomes a root of our social evils?
5. Do you agree that the love of money has a tendency to corrupt our religious life? Can you give illustrations of this from your own experience?
6. Why is the possession of wealth apt to involve the temptation to pride and arrogance?
7. Show that trust in riches is apt to make difficult a life of trust in God.
8. How is it that covetousness becomes an idolatry? Do you consider covetousness a dangerous idolatry in the modern world?
9. What does Paul mean when he says that no covetous man "hath any inheritance in the kingdom of Christ and of God"?
10. Is it possible for a man to become so absorbed in the pursuit of material things that he fails to lay hold of eternal life?

CHAPTER IX

The Dedication of Wealth to the Building of the Kingdom of God

The Renunciation of Wealth

AS we thought of the love of money as the root of all kinds of evil, we were naturally concerned with the spiritual perils involved in the getting and spending of money. As we analyzed this subject we saw that the love of money was one of the roots of almost every great social evil. We saw also the spiritual perils involved in the possession of wealth. We saw that men could become so absorbed in the riches of this world that they could not enter the Kingdom of heaven and lay hold of the life which is eternal.

Strange as it may seem to the members of our Protestant Churches today, when the quest for eternal life has been taken in utter seriousness it has often involved in the past the complete renunciation of the ownership of wealth. In the ancient church and in the Middle Ages, there were many orders of Christians in which the taking of the vow of poverty was a condition of membership. A similar vow is required of the members of many orders within the Roman Catholic and Greek Orthodox Churches today. This solution of the problem of a Christian's relation to material wealth was found in particular in the great institution of monasticism, which flourished for a long time as one of the ways of seeking to realize on earth the meaning of the Christian life. It is easy to see how this interpretation of the meaning of being a Christian flourished against the background of the evils of paganism and the awareness of the spiritual perils involved in the handling of money. The monastic orders, however, did not really escape from the problem of a Christian attitude toward the handling of wealth. The members of these orders did not own property as individuals. But the orders entered at once into the field of creating and accumulating wealth. In many cases the monks in their group relationships fell into all of the sins of avarice which had formerly characterized individuals who were dominated by covetousness.

The solution of the Christian's attitude toward wealth by the renunciation of all possession of wealth is not a solution that is true to the insights of Paul. Such a renunciation is possible only to those who do not bear a responsible relationship to others who are dependent upon them; i. e., to those who do not stand within the family relationship. For this reason the vow of poverty was usually connected with the vow of celibacy. A man could not take the vow of poverty when he faced the responsibility of having to provide for a wife and children. And in the end the vow of poverty usually involved a man's avoidance of the elemental responsibility of providing for his own needs. It is a good Pauline injunction that every man should seek to minister to his own necessities and to provide for those of his own household.[1]

God Giveth Us Richly All Things to Enjoy

When we think more deeply into this subject we must realize that the whole philosophy that undergirds monasticism is foreign to the thought of the Apostle Paul. This is an attitude toward life which was brought into Christanity from Greek and Oriental sources. It does not root in the Jewish and Christian tradition. In warning Christians against the perils of a false trust in riches, Paul tells them to trust in "the living God, who giveth us *richly all things* to *enjoy*."[2] We have here the understanding that God is the source of all the things which we, as Christians, enjoy. We must put our trust in God because it is God who gives us the things we enjoy. But we have here also the understanding that the good things of this life are to be *enjoyed*. Paul would have been willing at any time to endure hardness as a good soldier of Jesus Christ. But he would not have urged Christians to abstain from the normal pleasures of life when these did not conflict with the service of God. He warned the Colossians against any interpretation of Christianity which made them again subject to ordinances such as "Touch not; taste not; handle not," and he reminded them that such ordinances had indeed a "show of wisdom in will-worship, and humility, and severity to the body," but he asserts that they are of no value against the indulgence of the flesh.[3]

---

[1] Acts 20:34 and I Timothy 5:8.
[2] I Timothy 6:17.
[3] Colossians 2:21-23. (American Standard Version.)

In a similar vein, Paul in I Timothy condemns those who forbid to marry and who command to abstain from meats. He asserts that these are things to be received with thanksgiving of them which believe and know the truth. He broadens this statement to say that "every creature of God is good, and nothing is to be rejected, if it be received with thanksgiving: for it is sanctified through the word of God and prayer." And he tells Timothy that if he puts the brethren in remembrance of these things he will be a good minister of Jesus Christ.[4]

We have here an attitude toward life that is sane and wholesome. The Christian should receive with thanksgiving the good things which God so richly gives. There is no religious value in abstaining from meats for conscience' sake.[5] The joys which are connected with love, marriage, and the family life are to be part of the normal and happy experience of the Christian. These things are to be entered into in harmony with the understanding of them expressed in the Word of God. At times, Christians may be called upon by reason of some peculiar situation to renounce marriage. But this must never be exalted into the idea that the unmarried life is holier than the life that is possible within the marriage relation. The Christian should enjoy the good things that are to be found in the realms of art, literature, and music. The conveniences of modern life are to be accepted as setting men free from the drudgery of life and enabling them to give their time to the more creative things of life. These things should be received with thanksgiving. Paul is stern in his demands for *holiness*, but he does not stand for *asceticism*. He does not believe that through self-torture or self-denial a man can discipline himself until he reaches a high state of holiness.[6]

When we apply these general ideas to the whole matter of the Christian's relation to wealth we can see that for the Christian to seek to avoid the perils of wealth by seeking to embrace poverty is not a solution of our problem but a flight from it. In monasticism, the Christian ceased trying to live as a Christian in the midst of an evil world. He fled from the real world to an unreal world of his own making in which he sought to realize the meaning of the Christian life. But Christ's ideal for His followers is that they shall be *in*

[4] I Timothy 4:3-6. (American Standard Version.)

[5] We are not raising here the whole question of abstaining from meats offered to idols out of respect for the scruples of weak Christians.

[6] One of the criticisms of Jesus was that He came eating and drinking and that there was in Him no trace of the ascetic. (Matthew 11:19.)

the world but not *of* the world.[7] He does not pray that they shall be taken out of the world but that they shall be kept from evil. Christians who are to live in the world and to assume responsible relations in the world in which they live will inevitably be forced to have and to handle money. And the Christian attitude toward wealth does not lie in the renunciation of all wealth but in the will to use wealth in a way that is Christian.

The Temporal in the Light of the Eternal

Christianity gives to men an understanding of life which enables them to see the whole question of material possessions as they are set in a true perspective that is born of the Christian belief in the life beyond the grave. Paul knows the narrow limits within which material goods can minister to the needs of man. He writes to Timothy, "We brought nothing into this world, and it is certain we can carry nothing out."[8] In the Christian understanding of the life of man, the narrow limits that lie between the cradle and the grave are merely the beginning of the total span of man's life. To the Christian, the period of man's life in this world is a time of testing and preparation for the life that lies beyond this present world in the world of God which is revealed in the resurrection of Jesus Christ.

Jesus has given classic expression to this thought in the parable of the rich fool.[9] In this parable Jesus pictures the rich fool as he says to his soul, "Soul, thou hast much goods laid up for many years; take thine ease, eat, drink, and be merry." And in contrast to the word of the man to his soul, Jesus sets the divine word, "Thou fool, this night thy soul shall be required of thee: then whose shall those things be, which thou hast provided?" This remains one of the great unanswered questions of Scripture. Man can lay up treasure for himself. These treasures may be used to minister to some of his needs during the period which lies between the cradle and the grave. But no man is able to carry with him into the great beyond the material treasures which he has accumulated within his earthly pilgrimage. And Jesus gives the universal application of this parable as He says, "So is he that layeth up treasure for himself, and is not rich toward God."

---

[7] John 17:15, 16.
[8] I Timothy 6:7.
[9] Luke 12:16-21.

What we do not always understand is that the relevancy of this whole parable depends upon the Christian understanding of life. We cannot talk about a man's using his treasure to be rich toward God unless he believes in the existence of a personal God. There is no point in the words, "This night thy soul shall be required of thee," unless we believe in a judgment in which "we shall all stand before the judgment seat of Christ."[10] If a man is an atheist he can have no understanding of what is involved in using his goods to lay up treasure in heaven. If a man does not believe in the survival of life after death, he cannot understand what Paul is talking about when he speaks of using our material goods in such a way that we shall lay hold of eternal life. If a man has no understanding of spiritual riches, he can hardly afford to neglect material riches. Here again we run into the oft forgotten truth that a Christian philosophy of the use of wealth must root in the whole Christian understanding of life.

Godliness with Contentment

Because Paul does have the Christian view of life as a whole, he can urge Christians to seek, if necessary, to achieve contentment with very little. He condemns as destitute of the truth all those who suppose that godliness is a way of gain. But he does know that godliness with contentment is great gain.[11] And because he knows that they will not be able to take their material possessions with them when they leave this world, Paul urges his followers to be content if necessary with food and raiment.[12]

The goal of Christian character which Paul sets here needs to be realized afresh in the modern world. For a long time to come it will probably be true that the rich are comparatively few in number and that most people will have to seek to realize the meaning of the Christian life against the background of limited resources. Paul would urge all such to seek to combine godliness with contentment. If a man has learned to live on a comparatively limited income in such a way as to achieve inner peace and contentment, he is much richer than those who are so consumed by the passion for wealth that they know neither rest, nor inner peace, nor contentment. And it is possible for Christians, if necessary, to realize contentment with

---

[10] Romans 14:10.
[11] I Timothy 6:5, 6.
[12] I Timothy 6:8.

comparatively little of this world's goods because Christians have a view of life in which the things that money can buy are seen in their true perspective. In a world which may be described as money-mad, Christianity can perform to many people no greater service than that of teaching them to achieve contentment with the external circumstances which are part of their lot in life. In a world in which most people are dominated by false values, Christianity can teach men to realize the riches that are involved in character, in righteousness, in inner peace, in the loving service to others, and in that vast realm of spiritual values which make life worth while. In a world which thinks largely in terms of material things, Christianity can point out the perishing nature of all the things that belong to this present world and the abiding realities to be found in the things which are not seen but are eternal.

I Know How to Abound

But while Paul would teach the Christian to achieve, if necessary, contentment with the bare necessities of life, he would not shirk the responsibility of trying to teach those who are rich how to use their wealth in a way that is pleasing to God. In Philippians, Paul says of himself, "I have learned, in whatsoever state I am, therewith to be content. I know both how to be abased, and I know how to abound: every where and in all things I am instructed both to be full and to be hungry, both to abound and to suffer need. I can do all things through Christ which strengtheneth me."[13] In these verses, Paul says that he himself has personally learned the lesson of achieving contentment with the state in life in which he finds himself. As a part of this total experience, he has learned to so rely upon Christ for strength that he has achieved contentment in the midst of poverty or even in the presence of hunger. He knows the experience of being abased, of being in want, of suffering need, of being in actual hunger. He has found that he has in Christ spiritual resources to enable him to bear these conditions as a Christian. And in the same way, Paul is sure that a man can find in Christ the spiritual resources that will enable him to handle wealth in a way that is Christian. Because the Christian can do all things through Christ who strengthens him, Paul is sure that the Christian can learn to so handle the riches of this present world that he lays hold of eternal life. It may be im-

[13] Philippians 4:11-13. See page 87.

possible for those who *trust* in riches to be saved. But it is not impossible for those who have been *trusted* with this world's goods to be Christian in their administering of the wealth that has been committed to them.

That They Do Good

Paul does not work out in detail the way in which the rich must use their wealth if they are to be Christian in their attitude toward their possessions. But he does suggest in his charge to Timothy the general principles which must guide the rich in their use of their wealth in harmony with the insights of the Christian faith. We have noticed in our last chapter Paul's consciousness of the spiritual perils involved in the possession of wealth. He has told Timothy to warn the rich against the sins of pride or of a false trust in riches. He approaches the positive side of the problem when he tells Timothy to "charge them that are rich in this world . . . *that they do good, that they be rich in good works,* ready to distribute, willing to communicate; laying up in store for themselves a good foundation against the time to come, that they may lay hold on eternal life."[14]

Paul would charge the rich in this present world that they do good. This expression need not be limited to the good that the rich can do with their money. Every Christian, regardless of whether he be rich or poor, must seek to do what good he can as he passes through his earthly pilgrimage. And those who are rich may often do more through the personal use of influence, through teaching, through counseling, through the work of evangelism, etc., than they do through the use of their money. But in the setting in which we find it here, Paul's charge to the rich unquestionably refers primarily to the good that they can do with their money. The false love of money may become the root of almost every kind of social evil. But when wealth is controlled by those who are controlled by Jesus Christ it is possible for this wealth to be used as the means of doing good.

A Christian's capacity to do good as he passes through his earthly pilgrimage is enormously increased if in the providence of God he is entrusted with the control of large wealth. In the end, wealth represents stored-up human energy. And the man who controls wealth can release human energy for the great positive and constructive tasks which are a part of the building of the Kingdom of God.

---

[14] I Timothy 6:17-19.

We have already thought of these tasks in our chapters on "Fellowship in Ministering to the Saints" and "Fellowship in the Furtherance of the Gospel." We do not need to state them again in detail here. Wealth can be dedicated to Christ and used to minister to the needs of suffering humanity. The hungry can be fed. The naked can be clothed. The sick can be ministered to. Churches can be built. Hospitals and schools can be established and supported. The great causes of Home and Foreign Missions can be undergirded with adequate financial support. We do not need to elaborate this point. The details of the Christian use of wealth must be worked out in the light of the total needs of the Kingdom of God at any given time in world history. But every Christian who is entrusted with the control of wealth must face the question as to whether he is using his wealth selfishly or is administering it in an effort to do good. And Paul's first charge to the rich is that they shall use their wealth to do good.

In the closing scene of Scott's "Lady of the Lake" the poet describes the way in which the king uses his power to bring happiness to Ellen, to her father, the exiled Douglas, and to her lover, the imprisoned Malcolm. As he contemplates the joy which comes to the heart of James Fitz-James in this use of his power, Scott writes,

> "The Monarch drank, that happy hour,
> The sweetest, holiest draught of Power,—
> When it can say with godlike voice,
> Arise, sad Virtue, and rejoice!"

In a similar way the sweetest and holiest joy that goes with the possession of wealth is to be found in the power to do good that it places in the hands of those who control it. Those who control great wealth can speak with almost godlike voice in their capacity to minister to human need. We have thought in our last chapter of the love of money as a root of every kind of evil. But no Christian need be ashamed of the love of money if his desire for money is rooted in his yearning to increase in this way his capacity to do good. The love of money may be a holy desire when it is found in the heart of those who seek wealth that through it they may do good. The most consecrated Christian cannot be without some knowledge of the power of money to increase his capacity to do good. And the rich of the earth will find that through a wise use of their money in the effort to do good they drink the sweetest and holiest draught of the power of wealth.

That They Be Rich in Good Works

Paul charges those who are rich in this world's goods that they be rich in good works. Riches can be so used that those who possess them become "rich in good works." There is nothing unchristian in a man's use of his wealth to minister to his own needs and to the needs of those who are dependent upon him. There is nothing wrong with the setting aside of a certain amount of money so as to make provision for sickness, for old age, for dependents, etc. But it is much more Christian for a man to use his wealth to become rich in good works than it is for him to be primarily concerned to lay up treasure for himself and unconcerned about becoming rich toward God. And when a man over a period of time has used his wealth to do good in the name of Christ he comes to the place where he himself is rich not merely in the riches of this present world, but also in the good deeds which he through his money has wrought in the name of Christ. By this form of spiritual alchemy the riches of this present world can be transmuted into the spiritual riches that abide.

Ready to Share
Willing to Sympathize

Paul charges the rich that they be "ready to distribute, willing to communicate." The meaning of the first expression is clear. It refers to a man's readiness to share what he has with the need of others. What is the meaning of the expression "willing to communicate"? The American Standard Version gives as an alternate translation, "ready to sympathize." This translation probably suggests the real meaning of the phrase. The Apostle John writes, "But whoso hath this world's good, and seeth his brother have need, and shutteth up his bowels of compassion from him, how dwelleth the love of God in him?"[15] John warns the Christian who has this world's goods against the tendency to shut up his bowels of compassion when he sees that his brother has need. Paul expresses the same thought when he says that the Christian who has this world's goods must be "ready to sympathize." As Christians move in the presence of human need,

[15] I John 3:17.

they must fight constantly the tendency to harden their sympathies, or to shut up the bowels of their compassion.

Laying Up . . . Against the Time to Come

Paul charges the rich that they should be "laying up in store for themselves a good foundation against the time to come." We cannot be absolutely certain as to just what Paul means by urging Christians to lay up for themselves a good foundation against the time to come. It is, for example, not perfectly clear as to what he means by "the time to come." But in harmony with the whole movement of this passage the probability is that Paul here is referring to that time when every Christian must stand before Christ and give an account to Him of the deeds done in the flesh. Here again the Christian is set in sharp contrast to the rich fool in the parable of Jesus. The man in the parable has laid up treasure for himself until he can say to his soul, "Soul, thou hast much goods laid up for many years." He has not thought much about being prepared for that time when God will say unto him, "This night thy soul shall be required of thee." But to every man there is coming a time when he must give an account unto God of his stewardship. Every Christian will have to receive the judgment of Christ as to how he has handled the material possessions that have been entrusted to his keeping during the period of his earthly pilgrimage. The man who has used his wealth to do good has also used his wealth to be prepared for the time when he will be called upon to give an account of his stewardship.

Laying Hold on Eternal Life

Paul tells Timothy to charge those that are rich in this present world that they so handle their riches that they may "lay hold on eternal life." The American Standard Version translates this expression, "that they may lay hold on the life which is life indeed." But the two expressions have practically the same meaning. Paul is talking here about our capacity to lay hold of the eternal life which is the Christian's inheritance in Jesus Christ. How is it that Christians who are rich in this present world can use their wealth to lay hold of eternal life? In a negative sense we have here again a warning against that absorption in the things of this world which keeps us out of the Kingdom of heaven. The culmination of our last chapter was reached in that experience in which men were so dominated by covetousness that they could not enter the Kingdom of heaven. We have a vivid illustration of the power of wealth to come between men and Jesus Christ as the rich young ruler comes to Jesus seeking to find what he must do to inherit eternal life and turns away sorrowful because he has great possessions.[16]

When we ask the question as to how a Christian can use his riches to lay hold of eternal life, we must understand at once that Paul would be fundamentally opposed to any idea that men can use their money to buy eternal life or that any man can become so rich in good works as to merit salvation. The heart of Paul's preaching was found in his message of salvation by grace alone. Men lay hold of eternal life as they give up all trust in themselves or in their own righteousness and put their trust entirely in what God has done for them in Jesus Christ.

Laying Up Treasure in Heaven

But when the Pauline conception of salvation has been stated in all of its force, we must remember that there is nothing unchristian in urging men to so live in this life that they shall have treasure in heaven. Jesus urged His followers to seek to lay up for themselves treasures in heaven where neither moth nor rust would corrupt and where thieves would not break through and steal.[17] And in line with this injunction is it not possible for men to use their treasures upon earth in such a way that they shall have treasure in heaven? As we understand the meaning of the Christian gospel, a new seriousness enters into our earthly decisions. The man who uses his wealth to build a church in a needy section may help to set in the heart of a community an institution through which the doors of the Kingdom of God are opened to many. The man who dedicates his wealth to

---

[16] Mark 10:17-27. (Jesus saw that in the case of this man his wealth was the thing that stood between him and the laying hold of eternal life. And Jesus laid His hand fearlessly on the need of this man and demanded from him a renunciation of his wealth as the test of his readiness to become a disciple. But there is no indication that Jesus ever expanded His demand on this man into a general principle in which He made the taking of the vow of poverty a condition of discipleship. Jesus does demand a complete surrender of life to Him which would leave Him the Lord of our possessions even as He is the Lord of our lives. There is nothing in the teachings of Jesus which is out of harmony with the charge that Paul gives to the rich in this present world.)

[17] Matthew 6:19.

missons or to Christian education may set in movement influences which are eternal in their significance. It may be that it is only in the light of eternity that we can measure all of the good that may be accomplished by the wise dedication of wealth to the great causes of the Kingdom of God. The Christian who has consistently used his wealth to do good may go out into the great beyond with the consciousness that during his earthly pilgrimage he has been busy laying up treasure in heaven. In this sense, there may be truth in the statement that the dead take with them in their clenched grasp only that which they have given away.

Both in this life and in that which is to come, a man's capacity to receive the richest gifts which God has for His children may be related to the stewardship which he rendered of the material possessions that were trusted to him during his earthly pilgrimage. Did not Jesus say, "If therefore ye have not been faithful in the unrighteous mammon, who will commit to your trust the true riches?"[18] Did not Jesus in the great parable of the last judgment show the connection between the invitation, "Come, ye blessed of my Father, inherit the kingdom prepared for you from the foundation of the world," and the way in which those to whom this invitation is addressed have fed the hungry, visited the sick, clothed the naked, and ministered to those in prison?[19]

The Fine Art of Christian Stewardship

The practice of Christian stewardship is a fine art. It cannot be solved by the complete renunciation of the ownership of material possessions. It can only be solved as Christians use their possessions in a way that is Christian. And there is no simple rule which can guide the Christian in the best use of his possessions. The art of Christian stewardship requires a fine sense of balance and proportion. It roots in the whole Christian understanding of the meaning and purpose of life. It involves the spending of money to provide for our own necessities and for the needs of those who are dependent upon us. It involves a reasonable provision for the hazards of life —for sickness, unemployment, old age. It involves the wise use of money for the enrichment of life in terms of education and culture. In many cases a man increases his capacity to serve as he himself

[18] Luke 16:11.
[19] Matthew 25:31-46.

seeks for educational, cultural, and spiritual enrichment. Christian stewardship involves a sense of proportion between what we spend on ourselves and what we give to the causes of the Kingdom. It involves also a sense of proportion between the more immediate ministry to human needs and the great constructive tasks which ultimately strike at the heart of human need. Christian stewardship requires also a sense of values, a sense of proportion and balance between things temporal and things eternal. It will always be true that one of the most difficult tasks facing a Christian will be to be a Christian in his use of his money, to hold in a true balance the various demands made upon him, and to render a stewardship of his possessions which will be pleasing to God. Christian stewardship is an art. It is a difficult art to master. But those who master this art will find that they receive full compensation when they stand in the presence of their Lord and receive His, "Well done, good and faithful servant; thou hast been faithful over a few things, I will make thee ruler over many things: enter thou into the joy of thy Lord."[20]

---

[20] Matthew 25:23.

QUESTIONS ON CHAPTER IX

1. Show that some Christians have interpreted the quest for eternal life in terms of the complete renunciation of wealth.
2. What was the relation between the vow of poverty and the vow of celibacy?
3. Criticize from the point of view of the Apostle Paul the attempt to interpret Christianity in terms of the complete renunciation of wealth.
4. Show that Christianity gives us a philosophy of life in which our material possessions may be viewed in the light of our eternal destiny
5. How does our Christian faith enable us to combine godliness with contentment?
6. What does Paul mean when he says, "I know . . . how to be abased"?
7. Is it possible for Christians to find in Christ the power to achieve contentment in the midst of very limited material resources?
8. What does Paul mean when he says, "I know how to abound"?
9. In your opinion is it more difficult to be Christian in the midst of poverty or in the midst of wealth? How do you think Jesus would have answered this question?
10. Summarize the charge to the rich which Paul commits to Timothy.
11. How is it possible for the rich to find joy in the use of their wealth?
12. How can the rich become "rich in good works"?
13. How can we use our wealth within this world so as to prepare for the day of judgment which comes at the end of life?
14. How can we so use our earthly treasures that we lay up treasures in heaven?
15. Show that the practice of Christian stewardship is a fine art.

CHAPTER X

The Form of the Economic Order

Assuming the Form of the Economic Order

MOST Christians simply assume the economic order in which they move. They accept it without question even as they accept many of the other conditions within which the life of man upon our earth must be lived. Most Christians accept the economic order even as they accept the universe itself. The economic order into which they are born is to them the God-given framework within which they must seek to realize the meaning of the Christian life. And for the vast majority of Christians this attitude of the acceptance of the outer form of the economic order is wholesome. The individual Christian cannot begin at once to change the foundations of the order of life within which he lives. He cannot alter at once the whole environment of his life. His task is to assume this environment and to seek within it to be a Christian.

The movement of this book as a whole has been pitched on this plane. Paul did not call in question at once all of the foundations of ancient society. He sought to win men to a living faith in Christ. He sought to guide his converts into the realization of the meaning of the Christian life in the world of the first century. In a similar way, this book is not written to the scholars who sit apart and meditate on the way in which Christianity will ultimately transform society. It is written for men and women who must seek to be Christian in the world in which they must live now. It has sought to supply a philosophy of stewardship which can serve as a guide to people in the decisions they must make now. The book is written against the background of the economic order that exists today. It seeks to understand the great Christian insights concerning the getting and spending of wealth. It seeks to bring them to bear on the Christian conscience now.

Differing Forms of the Economic Order

Most Christians accept without question the outer form of the economic order within which they live. But every Christian must be at least dimly aware of the existence of the other forms of the economic order which by their very existence raise some questions about the form of the economic order within which he lives. There are few Christians, for example, who have not heard of the great experiment of communism in Russia. The Christian in America may have very dimly formed ideas concerning what this experiment means. Or he may have reached clearly formulated convictions concerning the good and the bad in the Russian form of the economic order. In either case, the very fact that millions of men do live under an economic order which is radically different from our own must raise even in the mind of the most unthinking Christian some questions as to the permanence of the form of the economic order within which he lives.

A Changing Economic Order

Most Christians are also aware that the economic order which they know is not entirely static. The capitalism of America today is not identical with the rugged individualism which characterized the life of the early pioneers of America. And the economic order of America is even farther removed from the feudalism which characterized the life of the Middle Ages or the slavery which was the prevailing form of the economic order in the world that Paul knew. The Christian is also aware that the world that he knows is changing. Even in America we have today a regimentation of life which our fathers of a generation ago would have considered an invasion of their sacred rights. The economic order is in process of change. The question before our generation is not so much the question as to whether the economic order will be gradually changed. The real question before us deals with the nature of the forces that will mold the economic order as it is gradually altered to suit the needs of a changing world.

Building the Builders of the Economic Order

The spread of the Christian faith will inevitably have its effect upon the functioning of the economic order. And in many ways this effect will be felt entirely apart from any attempt to call in question the foundations upon which the economic order rests. It is the function of the church to build the builders of the economic order. Ultimately the functioning of any order of society rests upon the character of the men who administer it. This is particularly true in the world of business. Business depends on credit. Credit in the end roots in character. Over a long period of time we cannot effectively deal with people unless we can trust them. The whole functioning of our present economic order roots in the fact that most men are honest. And when the fabric of an order of society becomes permeated with corruption, that society is heading toward a collapse.

A man's character roots in his whole attitude toward life. In the last analysis, it is the product of his religious faith. We would not deny that men of unquestioned integrity can be found who have little interest in religion. We are equally willing to admit that many of those who profess a faith do not live up to the demands of their creed. These considerations do not affect the general truth that the character of a man is rooted in his faith in the meaning and purpose of life. From this point of view, there is no greater task before the church than that of thrusting into society men whose integrity is rooted in foundations that will stand. When a man yields his life to Jesus Christ something happens at the core of his life. The Christian graces appear in lives that are rooted in the Christian faith. Christian conversion should work itself out in the renewal of the characters of men.

The church must build the men who build the economic order. And the need for men of character to administer the economic order will increase rather than diminish as humanity moves forward into the changing forms of the economic order. One result of the whole industrial revolution is an increasing centralization of power in the hands of a comparatively few men. But the more power a man wields the more important it becomes for him to use power with a high sense of stewardship. Humanity seems to be moving toward the increasing socialization of certain forms of industry. And the complex society of the modern world seems inevitably to involve a regimentation of life which was unknown in the simpler forms of society. The functions of government seem to be constantly expanding in the modern world. It is not our purpose here to evaluate these trends of society. All that we wish to say here is that all of these trends put an increasingly high premium on the importance of finding men who can be trusted when they are placed in positions of power. It is our conviction that society will not find the men who will be able to resist the temptations that go with power unless these men have been brought to yield their lives to a POWER that is greater than they are.

Examining the Sources of Our Wealth

A great and purifying principle is set in the midst of the economic order when we insist that every man who is a Christian must examine from the point of view of the insights of the Christian faith the sources of his wealth. In our study of the love of money as the root of all evil we saw the way in which false attitudes toward the getting of money could become the roots of almost every kind of social evil. If Christians would look more carefully to the sources of their wealth, they would strike at the roots of much of the evil that goes on in our national life. It would be generally conceded that every Christian must avoid the grosser forms of dishonesty in connection with the accumulation of his wealth. But there are many places in our national life at which the Christian conscience needs to be made more sensitive to the demands of the Christian ethic. If Christians today would analyze the sources of their wealth from the point of view of the demands of the Christian ethic, they would probably find many places at which the existing situation would need correction. But our interest here is not so much in the suggestion of the various places[1] at which the Christian conscience has been lax as it is in the statement of the general principle involved in our discussion as a whole. When men yield themselves to Jesus Christ, they must seek to make their wealth in a way that is pleasing to Him. It is the function of the church to bring this truth home to men and to lead men to study from a Christian point of view the sources of their wealth. We insist that this principle, if properly understood and applied, should become an elevating and purifying force in the midst of the economic order.

Being Christian in the Spending of Our Money

Christians should examine the sources of their wealth from the point of view of the demands of the Christian ethic. Alongside of

[1] See chapter on "The Love of Money As the Root of All Evil" for discussions of the various ways in which false attitudes toward wealth corrupt our social life.

this principle, we must set the equally important principle—a principle which the church must demand—that Christians should be Christian in the spending of their wealth. We must lay on the conscience of every man who is a Christian the pressure of the Christian understanding of the stewardship of wealth. A large proportion of the accumulated wealth of America is controlled by men and women who in name at least are Christian. Over against an irresponsible individualism in which every man has a right to spend his money as he pleases, we must set forth the Christian understanding of every man as responsible to Christ for the use that he makes of his money. Without altering at all the form of the economic order we could ameliorate its worst abuses if Christians would be Christian in the way they spend their money.

We have only made a beginning in this direction in North America, but we have made a beginning. In his little book, *Heritage and Destiny*, Dr. John Mackay points out the way in which leaders of South America are impressed by the extent to which great fortunes in America have been dedicated to the service of humanity. He says that a similar situation does not exist in the republics of South America. Many of the great fortunes of North America have been dedicated, in part at least, to the great causes of human welfare. But that which is at present exceptional enough to be news could become the accepted practice of Christians. And the real test of Christian stewardship comes not in the dedication of a few large incomes, but in the consistent practice of Christian stewardship by the great mass of Christians. If Christians would be Christian in their attitude toward the use of their wealth, they would lay the basis for the dedication of a large proportion of our accumulated wealth to the service of God through the service of man.

Christianity and the Present Form of the Economic Order

We have been considering the purifying effect on the economic order as a whole of the simple demand that Christians should be Christian in their getting and in their spending of wealth. But this demand must not be accepted as a substitute for a more fundamental process in which the existing economic order is judged in the light of the whole Christian understanding of man and his place in the universe. It is obvious that such an attempt to evaluate our economic life would run far beyond the demands of the study we are making now. All that we can do in this chapter is to suggest some of the lines along which such a study should move. As the first step in this process, we should make it clear that the Christian faith is not identified with the preservation of the existing form of the economic order. The Christian may tolerate the outer form of the economic order as the God-given framework within which he must seek to realize the meaning of the Christian life. But the Christian's attitude toward the economic order is far removed from the deification of the existing form of the economic order as the will of God for society. Clear thinking here is utterly essential for the guidance of the church in the social struggle. The church has a natural tendency to be conservative. The support of the church is usually tied up with the incomes of many of those who have a large financial stake in the preservation of the economic order. In such a situation there will always be pressure exerted upon the church to identify Christianity with the preservation of the economic order in its existing form. From this point of view, the history of Christianity often makes painful reading. Men have sought to throw the whole power of the church behind the preservation of slavery in America, or the tyranny of the feudalism of Russia, or the interests of the landed aristocracy of Spain. Christians need at this point to hear the words of Tennyson,

> "The old order changeth, yielding place to new,
> And God fulfills Himself in many ways,
> Lest one good custom should corrupt the world."

Christianity has lived with slavery, and feudalism, and capitalism. She may learn to live in the more socialized forms of society toward which modern society seems to be moving. In fact, she may find some of the newer forms of society more congenial to her life than the more ancient forms of the economic order. In this respect, Christianity must judge all orders of society. She must point to the evils in the existing economic order. She must be prepared also to examine from the point of view of the insights of the Christian any form of the economic order which may be established in the future.

Christianity and Some New Form of the Economic Order

This last statement leads us to another guiding principle of the church in the social struggle. If we insist that the church must not be identified with the existing form of the economic order, we must also insist that we must not identify Christianity with some proposed form of the economic order which is offered as a substitute for the evils of the world in which we live today. Sometimes a body of Christians will become so enthusiastic in their endorsement of some proposed substitute for the economic order which they now have that they will identify the bringing in of this order with the bringing in of the Kingdom of God. Such an identification is certain to be false. The new order as well as the old must be weighed in the balances of God. Within *every* form of the economic order, Christians must bear witness against the things that make it difficult for men to live Christian lives.

The Autonomy of the Economic Order

As they face the economic order, Christians must always be opposed to what is called the *autonomy* of the economic order. By the autonomy of the economic order we mean the tendency to consider the economic life of man apart from our whole view of the meaning and purpose of human life. We mean in particular the tendency of economics to escape from all moral and religious controls. The economic life of man is an important part of the whole life of man. The purpose of the economic order is to produce and to distribute the material goods which are to serve the needs of men. In this respect, the economic order ministers to a basic human need. And the economic life of a nation must be judged by the success with which it ministers to this need. Man cannot live without bread, but man cannot live by bread alone. And if we attempt to understand human life purely on the basis of economics we cannot even solve the problems of economics. Man is not merely the economic animal. Man is a child of God. Man is a being made in the image of God. And the economic life of man must be understood as the attempt of man, the child of God, to order his economic life in the interest of all of God's children and not in the interests of a privileged few. The economic order does not exist as an end in itself. It exists as a part of the larger life of man. As such it has a most important function to fulfill. And the ultimate success or failure of the way in which the economic order is functioning must be judged against the whole Christian understanding of man.

The Supremacy of the Profit Motive

As Christians consider the existing economic order they must object to the supremacy of the profit motive. The laborer is worthy of his hire. The man who works has a right to receive a fair return for his labor. This is true as much of the man who labors with heart and brain as of the man who works with his hands. And in the present organization of society the whole functioning of the economic order depends on the right of men to receive a fair return on their investments. But in much of modern society, whenever human rights have come into conflict with the demands for dividends, they have gone down with a regularity that is sickening. If we are going to continue to function within the capitalistic framework of society, we cannot destroy the right of men to expect a return on their investments. But the recognition of the profit motive is a different thing from the recognition of the *supremacy* of the profit motive. The demand for profits must not be asserted in such a way that the basic human rights are denied.

Labor as More Than a Commodity

In the same way, Christians must oppose the tendency to treat labor purely as a commodity. Labor is a commodity. In estimating the cost of an article to be placed on the market, men must estimate both the cost of the raw materials and the cost of labor. In this way the cost of labor becomes a most important part of the cost of the goods that are offered to the public. When labor is cheap and abundant and efficient, goods can be produced cheaply. When labor is scarce and inefficient, the cost of the production of goods will rise. Human labor is a commodity that is bought and sold in the market. But labor is much more than a commodity the price of which is to be determined merely by supply and demand; labor stands for the toil of human beings. The permanence of a man's job represents the permanence of his means of earning a living for himself and his family. The conditions under which a man works are a part of the standard of living which society creates for the workers of the world. The wage which a man earns affects his capacity to share in the fruits of the labors of other men. The final judgment against slavery as a form of the economic order was that under slavery human beings were treated like chattel to be bought and sold in the market. And within the modified capitalism of the western world we must not come to the place at which human labor is treated purely as a commodity. It is fair to say that most of the social legislation of recent years has sought to distinguish clearly between human labor and the other elements that enter into the cost of the finished product that is to be placed on the market.

Production and Distribution

Every form of the economic order must be judged by its capacity to bring about a fair distribution of the products of factory and farm. It is an unhealthy condition for the life of the nation as a whole when the control of the wealth of the nation becomes concentrated in the hands of a comparatively small number of families. When the rich grow richer and the poor grow poorer, the nation as a whole begins to suffer. During the days of the great depression, the fundamental problem of the nation was the problem of distribution. The industrial plants of the nation were able to produce the goods the people needed. The farms of the nation were able to produce the food the nation needed. At the same time the nation was faced by a vast unemployment problem which meant that millions could not purchase the basic necessities of life. The whole development of industry and science in the modern world has brought mankind to the place at which it is not physically impossible to banish want. Over a long period of time—with allowance for replacement of machinery and expansion of capital—the people of a nation can afford to consume what they are able to produce. The coming of the machine and with it the whole industrial revolution has placed mankind at the place where it is not inconceivable for the human race to produce enough to meet in a limited way the needs of all men. If it were possible for mankind to achieve a stable world order in which the energy of labor could be turned from producing the tools of destruction to the production of the things men need for a higher standard of living, it would not be physically impossible for men to produce the material goods that would greatly lift the standard of living of men all over the world. In the China of a generation ago, it was necessary for a large proportion of the population to live just above the starvation level. China did not have the tools or the skill with which to produce enough to meet the needs of her people. But it is not inconceivable that in another generation the Chinese people will be able to produce enough to enable all of their people to live in a degree of comfort that is impossible in the China of today. What we do not always understand is that the problems involved in the building of a world in which freedom from want can in large measure be realized are spiritual problems. The real question before our generation is whether the spiritual problems involved in building a world in which there is freedom from want can be solved. Within the economic life of North America, there is already much progress that has been made in the distribution of the products of industry. The standard of living of the masses of the people is probably higher than anywhere else in the world. But no one should be satisfied with the results that have already been achieved. Christianity does not set the goal of an equal distribution of wealth. Such a goal is neither possible nor desirable in a world in which men reap the fruits of their labor in the private ownership of wealth. But Christianity does envision a world in which there is something of an equality of economic opportunity. Christianity does envision a world in which the masses of the people have fair access to the means of acquiring and possessing property. Every form of the economic order must be judged both by its capacity to produce wealth and by its capacity to see that the fruits of labor are distributed with some degree of justice to those who produce them and to those who need them.

Summary

We have sought in this chapter to look at the economic order as a whole. We have sought to understand something of the impact of Christianity upon the economic life of man. We have seen that Christianity can move quietly as it transforms from within the spirit of the economic order. We have seen also that in the end the outer form of the economic order must be judged against the Christian insights concerning man and his place in the universe. We have seen that the Christian must distinguish between the ideal and the real. He must set for himself and for his world goals that are born of his understanding of the meaning of the revelation of God in Christ. At the same time he must face realistically the thing that is possible in the existing situation. It is along these lines that the full force of the gospel message must be felt in the economic life of man.

The Life of Man in the Light of God

In the ferment of modern society, the task of the church is to hold aloft the light of God, which is the only sure guide to the life of man. Woodrow Wilson spoke a great truth when he said that our civilization could not survive materially unless it was redeemed spiritually. There will never be roads where there ought to be roads, or bridges where there ought to be bridges, or factories where there ought to be factories, unless we keep alive in the hearts of men the knowledge of the eternal verities that are revealed to us in the coming of God in Christ. The task of building in the modern world an economic order which will truly serve the needs of man is a tremendous task—a task that calls for the noblest endeavor of the men of every generation. The problems of the economic order in the complicated life of the modern world will not be solved easily. They cannot be solved at all unless those who must face them look also to the ONE who has said, "I am the light of the world: he that followeth me shall not walk in darkness, but shall have the light of life."[2] It is only as the light of God falls on the life of man that we shall find the wisdom and the power to solve aright the problems of the economic order.

---

[2] John 8:12.

QUESTIONS ON CHAPTER X

1. Do most Christians raise fundamental questions about the righteousness of the form of the economic order in which they live?
2. Show that the first task of Christian stewardship is to guide people in their effort to live as Christians within the existing form of the economic order.
3. As contrasted to the capitalism of America, what other forms of the economic order have existed in the past? Are in existence today?
4. Show that the economic order within which we live is in constant process of change.
5. Why is it increasingly important for us to have as the builders of our economic order men of unquestioned integrity of character?
6. Do you agree that a man's moral character is the product of his religious faith?
7. How would the demand that men should be Christian in their attitudes toward the making of money act as a purifying force in its bearing on the whole economic order?
8. How would the demand that men should be Christian in the spending of their money work toward the dedication of wealth to high and worthy aims? To what extent is this process already at work in America?
9. Should Christianity ever be identified with the existing form of the economic order?
10. Why does the church have a tendency to be conservative in her social thinking?
11. Should the bringing in of the Kingdom of God ever be identified with the bringing in of some new form of the economic order?
12. Why is it necessary for Christians to oppose the autonomy of the economic order?

13. What do we mean by the supremacy of the profit motive?

14. Why is it that we cannot treat *labor* purely as a commodity?

15. Why is it that the efficiency of any form of the economic order must be judged both by its capacity to produce and by its capacity to bring about a fair distribution of the goods produced?

16. Why is it that man today for the first time in his history stands on the threshold of the possibility of banishing poverty and building an economy of abundance?

17. What do we mean when we say that the problems of the life of man can be solved only as they are seen in the light of God?

Appendix I

THE TEACHINGS OF SAINT PAUL CONCERNING CHRISTIAN STEWARDSHIP IN THEIR RELATION TO THE TEACHINGS OF JESUS

IN this book, I have given two chapters to the laying of the foundation for the study of the stewardship message of Paul. The first of these is devoted to the Old Testament background of Paul's thought. The second deals with the development of stewardship in the church before Paul assumed leadership in the Christian community. The necessity for both of these chapters is obvious. But a discerning critic is apt to ask why I did not give a third chapter in which I dealt with the relation between the teachings of Paul concerning stewardship and the teachings of Jesus on this same subject.

Jesus, in the days of His flesh, taught many things concerning the stewardship of possessions. His teachings will always remain our richest source of Biblical material for the preaching of stewardship. My reason for centering this book in the teachings of Paul does not root in any failure to appreciate the tremendous significance of the teachings of Jesus in the field of stewardship. I have chosen to study the teachings of Paul because the teachings of Jesus concerning stewardship have been carefully studied and the teachings of Paul have been neglected. There are many books that deal with one aspect or another of the teachings of Jesus in the field of stewardship. I do not know personally of a single full-length book that devotes itself exclusively to the teachings of Paul.

My purpose in this appendix does not include any attempt to discuss the significance for the church today of the teachings of Jesus on stewardship. I am limited here merely to an inquiry as to the relation between the teachings of Paul and the teachings of Jesus as they both deal with the subject of stewardship. I did not give a full chapter to this study, as I did not seem to be able to lay hold of any unifying idea which would give this chapter its proper place in the study as a whole. I do feel that a few comments should be given here in order that our study of the background of Paul's thinking concerning stewardship may be complete.

Are Paul and Jesus in agreement in their teachings concerning stewardship? Does Paul get his ideas concerning stewardship from Jesus or does he arrive at them independently? These and similar questions naturally come to us as we consider the relation between stewardship in the Pauline Epistles and stewardship in the Gospels.

The relation between the teachings of Paul and the teachings of Jesus on stewardship cannot be considered apart from an understanding of the whole relation between the preaching of Paul and the teaching of Jesus in the days of His flesh. When we examine the letters of Paul as a whole we must realize that we have in them only a limited number of references to the life and teachings of Jesus apart from the consummation of the ministry of Jesus in His death and resurrection. In I Timothy 6:13, 14, Paul writes to Timothy, "I give thee charge in the sight of God, who quickeneth all things, and before Christ Jesus, who before Pontius Pilate witnessed a good confession; that thou keep this commandment without spot, unrebukeable, until the appearing of our Lord Jesus Christ." In the clause, "who before Pontius Pilate witnessed a good confession," we have a reference to the trial of Jesus before Pilate. This is a reference to an event in the life of Jesus, but as far as I have been able to discover it is the only reference of this kind (exclusive of the death and resurrection) to be found in the letters of Paul. And even here the background of this reference shows that Paul is thinking primarily of the risen Christ, who will return in glory and in power.

The references to the teachings of Jesus are almost as limited. In his speech before the elders of Ephesus, Paul, in a speech which Luke has preserved for us, refers to the words of the Lord Jesus, "It is more blessed to give than to receive."[1] In some of Paul's teachings, he distinguishes between his own advice and the word of the Lord.[2] But it is impossible to be sure here whether Paul is referring to a word of the Lord spoken in the days of His flesh, preserved in the church and passed on to Paul, or to a direct communication

---

[1] Acts 20:35.

[2] I Corinthians 7:10, 12, 25; 9:14; 14:37; I Thessalonians 4:15.

received by Paul from the risen Jesus. And in at least some of the instances it would seem that the latter interpretation would be the most natural understanding of Paul's language.[3]

We are unable to say, therefore, just how much of the teaching of Jesus which is preserved for us in the four Gospels was known to Paul. We do know that Paul had abundant opportunity to learn from those who knew it best the message of Jesus in the days of His flesh. He spent two weeks with Peter.[4] He conferred with James, the Lord's brother.[5] He knew John the apostle.[6] He was intimately associated with Barnabas. We know that Barnabas was associated almost from the beginning with the first Christian community at Jerusalem. The accepted tradition in the church is that the third Gospel goes back to Luke. Luke remained to the end a faithful friend of Paul.[7] It is difficult to believe that Luke did not share with Paul the information which he so carefully gathered concerning the things "which are most surely believed among us."[8] Paul knew also John Mark.[9] Mark was also a part of the early Christian community at Jerusalem. Peter calls him his son.[10] Mark is usually accepted as the author of the second Gospel. Paul spent two years at Caesarea.[11] The Christians there must have included many who had known Jesus in His earthly ministry.

For the reasons we have given, it is difficult to believe that Paul was not in some measure familiar with the teachings of Jesus which are recorded in the four Gospels, but Paul does not reveal this knowledge in his letters or in his speeches in Acts. The starting point of all his thinking was the crucified but risen Lord. He identifies the risen Christ with the Jesus of history.[12] But in the letters that have been preserved for us he makes very few references either to the words of Jesus or to the works of Jesus in the days of

[3] See especially I Thessalonians 4:15 for a reference to the word of the Lord which can hardly be a preservation of a teaching of Jesus in the days of His flesh.

[4] Galatians 1:18.

[5] Galatians 1:19.

[6] Galatians 2:9.

[7] Colossians 4:14; II Timothy 4:11; Philemon 24.

[8] Luke 1:1.

[9] Acts 12:25; 15:37, 39; Colossians 4:10; II Timothy 4:11; Philemon 24.

[10] I Peter 5:13.

[11] Acts 24:27.

[12] I Timothy 6:13.

His flesh. For this reason it is not possible to trace any very close and direct connection between the teachings of Paul concerning stewardship and the teachings of Jesus.

But the understanding of the independence of Paul's thought here makes all the more remarkable the basic agreement between Paul and Jesus. There is, however, a marked contrast in the way they present their teachings concerning stewardship. The teachings of Jesus are to be found in His discourses, in interviews such as the scene with the rich young ruler, and most of all in His parables. The interest of Jesus centers in a man's attitude toward wealth as it bears on his whole spiritual development. The actual needs of Jesus for money were limited to the simple needs involved in His own support and in the support of the band of apostles.

In contrast to the setting in which the teaching of Jesus is found, Paul is deeply involved in the task of actually building the world church. He is sending messengers all over the Roman Empire as a means of keeping in touch with the churches he has founded. He is planning missionary journeys into unevangelized territory. He is binding together through the offerings for the saints at Jerusalem the Jewish and the Gentile groups in the church. The actual situation which Paul faced has much in common with that which the church still faces as she gives herself to her world mission today. For this reason the advice of Paul has a certain relevancy to the situation of the church today which could not be fully expressed until the church actually entered upon her world task. The basis for the teaching of stewardship is to be found in the teachings of Jesus. But the practical application of these principles to the actual problems of the church is to be found in the letters of Paul.

Paul in his teaching concerning stewardship has a point of view which Jesus in the days of His flesh could not fully have. When Paul writes he can look back to the death, the resurrection, and the ascension of Christ. He sees the whole revelation of God in Christ, and he writes to the church that is founded on the witness of the apostles to these mighty works of God. This means that Paul can relate the giving of Christians to the full understanding of that which God has done for us in Jesus Christ. He can see all of our earthly life as there falls on it the light of God which is revealed in the death and resurrection of Christ. The full implications for Christian stewardship of the death and resurrection of Christ are implicit in the teachings of Jesus. They could not be made fully explicit until men could look back on the work of Christ and interpret its significance for all of Christian thought.

But when the differences in form, setting, and point of view have been pointed out, the deep unity in fundamental ideas which is to be found in the teachings of Jesus and the teachings of Paul is all the more remarkable. As we seek to set forth the thought of the Apostle Paul concerning stewardship, the stories of Jesus come to us at once as almost perfect illustrations of the ideas we are trying to present. Paul warns against putting our trust in uncertain riches rather than in God who gives us all things richly to enjoy.[13] Jesus tells the story of the rich fool.[14] Jesus in connection with the story of the rich young ruler warns against a trust in riches which makes it impossible for us to enter into the Kingdom of God. This story gives us a superb illustration of Paul's teaching in which he says that the covetous man cannot enter the Kingdom of God.[15] Paul tells the rich to be rich in good works, laying up a good foundation against the time to come.[16] Jesus tells the story of Dives and Lazarus.[17] Paul speaks of those who through the love of money have erred from the faith.[18] Jesus says that we cannot serve both God and mammon.[19] If we find our texts for our sermons on stewardship in the writings of Paul, we are almost certain to find our most effective illustrations in the life or in the teachings of Jesus.

This brings us again to our question as to the relation between the teachings of Jesus and the teachings of Paul in the field of stewardship. We cannot say whether Paul actually knew the teachings of Jesus which have been preserved for us in the Gospels. We can say that the unity between Paul and Jesus is not an accident. This unity is born of the complete surrender of Paul to the risen Christ whom Paul knew to be the same person as the Jesus of history. He who spoke to us in the days of His flesh spoke also through His servant whom He had chosen to bear His name "before the Gentiles, and kings, and the children of Israel."[20]

---

[13] I Timothy 6:17.
[14] Luke 12:16-21.
[15] Ephesians 5:5.
[16] I Timothy 6:18, 19.
[17] Luke 16:20-25.
[18] I Timothy 6:10.
[19] Matthew 6:24.
[20] Acts 9:15.

Appendix II

CONCERNING REFERENCES TO THE PASTORAL EPISTLES AND THE SPEECHES OF PAUL IN ACTS

IN some of the reviews of my book *The Social Teachings of the Apostle Paul,* I have been severely criticized because I refer to the pastoral Epistles as Pauline and use as source material for my study of the thought of Paul the speeches of Paul and the account of his life which are to be found in the book of Acts. As in this book I follow the same policy I feel that it is necessary to make a further word of explanation.

This is not the place for a discussion of the complicated problems involved in ascertaining the authorship of disputed books of the New Testament. I do not pretend to have made any exhaustive study of the authorship of the pastoral Epistles; i. e., I and II Timothy and Titus. I do know the usual arguments for and against the Pauline authorship of these books. Having examined these arguments I still feel that the weight of the evidence is in favor of the Pauline authorship. It would seem to me that the difficulties involved in the rejection of the Pauline authorship of these books would be considerably greater than the difficulties we have to face when we accept the Pauline authorship.

When we come to the book of Acts, we find that a consistent Christian tradition ascribes this book to Luke. There can be little doubt that Luke was closely associated with Paul. It would seem to me that Luke as the biographer of Paul could be counted upon to be as accurate in the picture he gives us of Paul in Acts as he is in the picture he gives us of Jesus in his Gospel. Would any man attempt to deal with the thought of Jesus without using the material in Luke's Gospel? And would it not be equally foolish to rule out Acts as a source for the study of the life of Paul? As a matter of fact, it is the narrative of the book of Acts that furnishes us an indispensable background for the study of the Epistles of Paul.

I cannot feel that disputes concerning the authorship of the Epistles of Paul are particularly important for a study of the message of Paul concerning Christian stewardship. Regardless of whether or not they have come entirely from the hand of Paul, in the form in which we now have them, the pastoral Epistles are accepted in the church as part of the canon. The passages in these letters which deal with stewardship represent insights concerning stewardship which are rooted in the whole experience of God in Christ that underlies the New Testament. They are part of the deposit of faith which is both the source and the norm of the thinking of the church. It is, therefore, entirely proper that we should turn to them for guidance for the thinking of the church concerning stewardship today. The book of Hebrews I do not regard as Pauline. But if this book contained some profound insights concerning stewardship not found elsewhere in the New Testament they could be treated in this study as a valid source for our study of the effort of the New Testament church to deal with the Christian use of wealth.

I do not feel that there is any lack of unity between the undisputed Epistles of Paul, the pastoral Epistles, and the book of Acts. The same towering figure of the great apostle lies behind them all. Through them Paul spoke to his generation, and through them he speaks to us today.

Bibliography

1. *Will a Man Rob God?* by Bishop Ralph S. Cushman. Abingdon-Cokesbury Press, Nashville.

2. *Save Money,* by John M. Versteeg. Abingdon-Cokesbury Press.

3. *The Stewardship Parables of Jesus,* by Roswell C. Long. Abingdon-Cokesbury Press.

4. *Stewardship,* by W. C. Morro. Christian Board of Publication, 2700 Pine Street, St. Louis.

5. *When Christ Controls,* by John M. Versteeg. Abingdon-Cokesbury Press.

6. *Achieving Results in Church Finance,* by Boyd M. McKeown. Abingdon-Cokesbury Press

7. *A Vital Christian Approach to Church Finance,* by Warren H. Denison. The Missions Council, Congregational Christian Churches, 287 Fourth Avenue, New York 10, New York.

8. *Royal Partnership,* by M. E. Melvin. Fleming H. Revell Company, 158 Fifth Avenue, New York, New York.

9. *Money the Acid Test,* by David McConaughy. The Westminster Press, Philadelphia.

10. *The Christian and His Money Problems,* by Bert Wilson. George H. Doran Company, New York, New York.

11. *A Man and His Money,* by Harvey Reeves Calkins. The Methodist Book Concern, New York, New York.

Index

Index